Poems

This volume is a collection
of all the published poems
of
Marjorie Pizer

PINCHGUT PRESS
Australia

This is the complete collection of Marjorie Pizer's published poetry, from her fifteen published works and other places. For 35 years she was a psychotherapist in Sydney. She now lives in Canberra.

Acknowledgements
Some poems in this collection have previously appeared in the *Bulletin, Sydney Morning Herald, Quadrant, Poet, Australian Women's Weekly, Cleo, Woman's Day, Education, Habitat* and in a number of anthologies of poetry published in the United Kingdom.

Cover: Ink drawing by Marjorie Pizer.
Back Cover: Ink drawing by Judy Lane
Cover Design: Kim Holburn

This edition first published in 2014
Version 1.1
Copyright ©Marjorie Pizer, 2014
Published by Pinchgut Press
11 Bates St, Canberra, Australia, 2602
http://www.pinchgut-press.com.au
Printed by Lulu http://www.lulu.com
ISBN 978-0-9871191-6-2

Foreword

The last book of poetry my mother published was *"A Poet's Life"*. She referred to it as the "definitive collection" of her poetry. I wonder if she knew at the time that she was not going to be able to continue writing.

As her son and literary executor, I get requests for her books occasionally. Many are out of print. I decided to publish this book for all those who, like me, love Marjorie's poetry. Here, then, is a complete collection of all her published poems.

Kim Holburn

This volume is published in dedication to my mother Marjorie Pizer. Born in 1920, she burned and raged against the darkness, most of her life but now is going gentle into that good night, unable to continue writing.

Contents

Gifts and Remembrances — 1979
153

To You, The Living — 1981, 1991, 1992
182

Bereavement and Loss
184

Thou and I — 1967

Only in my poems am I free
To speak of me.
I can say anything and I can be.
In my poems
I do not have to hide away
And keep the world at bay.
In my poems I am me,
And therefore, in my poems, I am free.

Remembrances

An old tape recording

When I think
That I might hear your voice
After four years of death,
My heart shrinks within me, –
Yet I must listen.
I must listen To that dead voice
Calling over the years
For hope and happiness,
For living unachieved –
And I must hush
My weeping heart
Even after all these years.

Memory

Sometimes I can hear your name
Almost without noticing.
But when she spoke your name
This morning
Suddenly I shrank inside,
Shuddering,
And I thought
Six years is only yesterday,
Sometimes,
Just when I am not expecting it.

Garden of Remembrance

(This garden has a rosebush for every man from the district killed in the past three wars)

Walk quickly past the roses,
Walk quickly past the names,
Walk quickly through the tears.
Do not remember the sons who are lost;
Do not think on the friends who will never return;
Do not remember the husbands who will never come back;
Do not recall the dreams undreamt,
The lives unlived,
The love unloved.
My eyes are full of tears –
I cannot read the names.

O gardener,
Why do you dig another bed
To plant more roses in?

(This poem was written during the Vietnam War)

Anniversary Lament for Joan

This time last year
The boy was here —
Painting the shed,
Going to bed.
This year no more
Will he pass the door,
Will he read a book,
Will he sit and look.
He is dead,
With all unsaid,
With little done, —
Your son.

Thoughts and Comments

Learning to paint

There is a body,
Lovely in line and shape,
Standing to be painted.
And here am I,
With every colour captured
And every shape to hand,
With loveliness enraptured,
Urgent to place it down,
To stamp that sight for other eyes to see.
Oh, struggle of hand and eye,
Of colour, vision and my inability.

How long before my fingers catch
The beauty of that figure there
And on this paper place its match?

On writing poems

Why do I wrestle with words so greatly,
Pushing this one here, changing that one there,
Turning this line around, making a new rhyme here.
Oh, intransigent and inadequate language of the English,
Why won't you say what I want to say?

Why does the thought change as it becomes word?
The feeling felt, how can it be said?
The looking looked, how can it be put?
The knowing known, how can I write it there?
O barrier of words, how can I make you mine?

An end and a beginning

To suddenly find that you have completed the struggle,
That you have left the agonising and the effort,
To find the surge of time no longer haunts the ear,
And that instead of an end,
There is a most beautiful of beginnings,
And a slowness and a loving and a let-beingness,
And a seeing of all the looked-for things. –
This is indeed a wonder and a quiet,
And a time for the growing of beauty in the heart.

To stand aside from the game and look

To stand aside from the game and look
Is different, is new.
To look at what people do
And not do it – this is true.
To be a stranger in the world of men –
This is suddenly the surprise.
To find that the rules aren't your rules any more
And you can see the lies –
This is wise.
To see the very beauty of it all,
And be apart, –
This is the new task of learning for the heart.

Committee meeting

How the past sits here in this room
Wrapping me round,
Wrapping the words and speeches,
Tying the problems up like old parcels.
Each person at the long table
Sitting in a cocoon of the past,
Tied by their thinking into narrow lanes
Quite undeviating.

Who is to break these chains?
Who is to cast this armour off
And speak the words of fire to free these souls?

"They"

When they say – that's wrong –
Do you question them?
When they say – that's bad –
Do you doubt them?
When they praise this –
Do you wonder why?
When they applaud that –
Do you follow them?
When they say – do this –
Do you do it?
When they say – don't think –
Do you say they know best?

Why do you always need a "they"
To send you safely on your way?

The mind

Who does the mind belong to,
O learned doctors?
Who does the mind belong to,
O wise psychiatrists?
The mind belongs to the philosopher,
To the thinkers and seers.
The mind belongs to the writers,
To the poets and the singers.
The mind belongs to the scientists,
The psychologists and the religious.
The mind belongs to every man,
To every woman and every child,
And perhaps it even belongs to God.
O possessive psychiatrists,
The mind does no belong to you.

For a group of mothers meeting in Sydney to discuss "The Feminine Mystique"

O mothers,
Sitting at the table
Wrestling with the problems of women –
How many centuries
Have your eyes been shut?
How many centuries
Have your minds been sleeping?
How many centuries
Have you been slaves and servants,
Wives and mothers and less than dust?
How many centuries
Have men and governments
Ordered your living and ordered your loving?

Only now are you beginning,
Slowly and proudly,
To be people.

Primitives

Long centuries ago
Virgins were sacrificed
To the gods of fear.
Today,
Being more civilised,
We sacrifice our young men
To the god of war.

Lakeside Holiday

Stillness of the morning,
Bellbirds belling,
Light silvering the lake,
And all are sleeping.
Curled in their beds,
The magic of sleep upon them,
They lie as beautiful as the lake,
Quiet and abandoned.

Moonlight

The magic of moonlight pouring down
Its incandescence on garden and home,
Bathing the silent sleepers there
In the silvering light of its shining hair.

What is your message,
O silent moon,
To the world all wracked
And out of tune?

This morning my car

This morning my car
Was covered with tiny flowers.
They had been falling for hours.
From afar
It looked like God had shaken the very tree
And blessed my car with special flowers for me.

Friendship

Morning Tea

When we sat in your kitchen drinking cups of tea,
No one would have thought we were doing anything important.
We were only talking, with our feet up on the chairs,
And you smoking a cigarette and hearing the rain outside.
But I was talking to you and you talking to me
And words weren't always needed.
We talked of many things, of birth and death,
And mother-in-laws and scrubbing floors,
Of our children and what to do in the garden,
And how people admire self-sacrifice,
And whether one has to work to live.
And when we had finished our tea,
We washed up the cups and saucers and were satisfied.

Not employed

What more could I wish for than this?
A chair in the warm sun of a winter's day
On the verandah of an old white house.
A sandwich of fresh bread with crisp crusts.
A cup of tea, brisk in the mouth,
The steam hot on my nose,
And my friend beside me talking,
Waiting for the children to come home for lunch. –

Yet some would have me work my days away
For the drab safety of each week's dull pay.

Winter

When I wake these mornings
The air is very cold,
And it is hard to get out of bed.
When I do get up,
I cook breakfast
And cut lunches for the children.
Then I have a shower,
Happy
Because I am spending the day with my friend.

Lunch party

When we got out of the car and went inside the house,
The ladies were waiting for us.
We had greetings and lunch and talk
And coffee with and without milk,
And we admired the room and the arrangement of plants outside the
         windows.
And nothing was said that was of the slightest importance to anyone.
Then we went away in the car, rejoicing,
Being together again,
And spoke of many other things.

When I looked up

When I looked up
And saw you at the gate,
I was pleased
That you had come to the house.

You looked so warm
In your heavy coat and brown gloves,
Bringing summer warmth
Into that winter's day.

A friend

Sometimes in your life
You hold out your hand to another,
Tentatively, carefully,
Wondering how close they can be,
Wondering how close you can let them be.
And you talk together,
And you walk together,
And you laugh together
For a long time.
And slowly there comes a time
When the armour is put aside
And the shield is unneeded,
And the two of you are just there,
Communicating.

And then, one day,
Suddenly, without warning,
There is your friend,
Fully helmed and braced,
Standing with sword in hand
Holding you off.
And then your heart curls up into a little ball,
Hurt and alone and very vulnerable.

Do not reach for your armour,
Do not arm yourself anew –
But reach out your naked hand
And speak your heart
Until the armour is shed again
And the sword is sheathed.

Feelings

Loneliness

To be with you is enough,
To be alone is enough.
To be lonely being alone
Is a restlessness.

Why do I hanker for the voice of a friend
At night in a lonely house,
When the children sleep?
Why do I look for a comforting hand
In the dark of the still house,
When the children are quiet?

Soul, give over your restlessness.
Soul, create you world in my house at night,
As you do in the light.

Retreat

Why does my spirit now and then
Fling itself down into the deep
Of despair?
Then I can only weep
For my own misery and wish
Myself alone.
Then I retreat into my own shell
And shut the world away
And have nothing to say.
And yet out there, all is well,
Sun shines, children play,
And I alone am out of tune.
Come, come my heart, be brave,
Fight through this anguish soon
And reach for life again.

For . . . .

How can you be so cold,
So efficient, so practical?
How can you be so icily capable
Sitting just there, in your chair?
— A comma goes here, a full stop goes there —
O, to be so efficiently clear,
Never a feeling, never a tear
On the other side of the table there.
Will anything shake you?
Will anything wake you
Sitting so tight, so apart?
Will anything touch you,
Wound you and warm you,
Will anything move your heart?

Dissatisfaction

Why am I dissatisfied with myself?
What is wrong?
I am angry with my children
For no good reason.
I did not speak to my friend
When she came to visit me.
I am trying to write a book
That is not being written.
I do not know
Whether my poems are worth reading.
I am not a good housekeeper
And my house is untidy.
There are ants in my kitchen
And books everywhere,
And I sit and read
When I should be working –
No wonder I am dissatisfied with myself.

When I am sick

When I am sick
The world is sad.
When I am well
The world is glad.

Our world is in us
As we smile or sigh,
But we pretend it is the world
That makes us laugh or cry.

Mind-at-large

What is it
I am touching up there?
What strange love is it
That washes like the sea
And touches all,
Even the unknowing.

On being different

To be different from all the rest
Is to be separated,
And to be separated
Is to be alone.

To be alone
Is to be frightened.
To be alone
Is to wonder if you are wrong.
To be alone
Is to wonder if they are right.
To be alone
Is to fight against the world.
To be alone and different
Is the beginning or the end of living.

Destruction and Creation

I have been to the edge of the abyss
And I have looked into the depths.
There I looked at death
And have returned to the living.
There I looked at madness
And have returned to the sane.
There I looked at destruction
And have returned to create.
For only creation and love
Can answer destruction and madness and death.

A message for my friend

My heart is cold and hard.
My love is withered away.
I don't care any more,
Just leave me alone.

Leave me alone in my house
With the wind and the rain outside,
With the cold rain in my heart,
And no wind to blow it away.

Leave me alone in my house
To mourn my withered heart.

For R. on her awakening

How beautiful it is
To shake awake
One who has lived with closed eyes,
With slumbering brain and unused voice
For all her life.

How beautiful it is
To reach a hand
And to see her banish fear,
To see her break the wall
Closing her lips and closing her mind.

How beautiful it is
To see the agony disperse
To see the eyes uncloud,
To see the hatred and the anger go
And see the person shimmering there below.

How very beautiful to see the flowering of a soul.

Love

Tonight the winter storm

Tonight the winter storm
Beats at my roof.
The wind heaves under the doors,
And I move close to the fire.

My children sleep,
And I wish — I wish
That you were here,
Keeping me company in this wilding storm.

When we are apart

When we are apart
Your presence surrounds me
Like an aureole
Around my heart
And goes with me continuously.

When we are meeting
My soul is fleeting
Swifter than body
And faster than light
To reach your sight.

And when we meet
In any room or street,
Our eyes give love to each
And hand in hand
We are specially blessed of all the land.

Size

When I lie with my head on your breast
And your arms around me,
I feel small and protected
By my beloved.

When you lie with your head on my breast
And my arms around you,
I feel so strong, protecting
My beloved

When I look at my bed

When I look at my bed
I am sad
That it is empty.
I am sad
That you are not there,
Curled up in my arms
Asleep.

Love

Loving you is so strange and intense
It cannot be said.
With you in bed
Nothing but love is of any sense.
Soul burns with soul in one,
Body with body tightly merge.
Passionate verge
Of oneness and who can see
Which is body and which is mind?
Which is you and which is me?
With this kind of loving are we both undone —
We cannot quench the shining of our sun.

To Life — 1969

Let me find poems everywhere I look

Let me find poems everywhere I look,
In friends, in trees or in a book.
Let poems come into my head
Saying whatever should be said.
Whatever I am doing, let me find
Poems coming into my mind.

Below the surface

What layer of living do you want to look at?
Do you want to slide over the surface
Or are you ready to dig deeper?
I am not satisfied with surfaces.
I need to see beneath the skin to the inmost bone.
I want to touch the very soul of another, —
I am not satisfied with the outside shell of his being.
I am not interested in the fronts he hides behind,
I want to find his very heart and mind.
If you are looking for me — I am here.
I, too, am looking for you.

Memories of childhood

O memory of childhood
Long since gone,
Returning to me now.
Only I could know
The anguish hidden below.
Only I could know
The secret love burning inside.
Only I could know
The grief I had to hide.
Today I cried for you,
That childhood me,
Tears from the years gone by,
Opening my heart anew.

For my mother

Mother means hate
And mother means love.
I think of my mother
And I am bitter at her rejection.
I weep inside for her lack of love
And I am sorry because I disapointed her.
I was difficult.
I was disagreeable.
I was not the daughter she had hoped for.
I wanted love
And I couldn't say so.
I wanted to be wanted
And nobody cared.
I wanted to be listened to
And nobody heard me.
O my mother,
If only you could have held out your hand to me
Once, just once,
Before you died.

What a burden of fears

What a burden of fears
We all carry.
What a sea of tears
We hide below the surface.
What hidden hates
Eat deep into our hearts.
No wonder our bodies are ill
With these emotions held so still
And pushed into the bones and flesh
So that they will be forgotten.
If only we could undo this mesh,
How free and beautiful we could be.

Sometimes

Sometimes
When I lie in my bed
And think of my life,
I am amazed that I am me.
How did I get here?
Is it really me in this house?
Sometimes,
When I lie in my bed
Just before sleep,
I am amazed that I am me.

A Father Dead

I cannot speak to my children about their father—
He is lost to them and to me.
There is an empty space where a father should be.
There is an empty space where a husband should be.
There is a sea of grief between me and my children
And I cannot speak of their father.
Perhaps they think that I have forgotten him
After all these years.
It is just that I cannot speak of him
Because of all these tears.

Muir

Six years you are dead
And sometimes I have almost forgotten.
Six years you are dead
And sometimes I cannot forget.
Sometimes you seem like a dream.
Sometimes I dream you
As if you are real.
Six years is a long parting
And still the memory is hurting.

The Existence of Love

I had thought that your death
Was a waste and destruction,
A pain of grief hardly to be endured.
I am only beginning to learn
That your life was a gift, a growing
And a loving left with me.
The desperation of death
Destroyed the existence of love,
But the fact of death
Cannot destroy what has been given.
I am learning to look at your life again
Instead of your death and your departing.

Lament

I am lamenting the loss of love in my life,
The friendships failed,
The friendships ended,
The family hardly known,
Father and brothers and mother,
Unreached, untouched.
I am lamenting the death of my beloved,
The ending that was not intended,
A man becoming a memory in a moment.
How my heart grieves for the dead ones
And the lost ones,
And how my heart leans out
To gather in those who are close to me.

Spring

Spring has come
And my cold heart is rising
With the sap. My winter sadnesses
And lonelinesses
Are fading in the slow awakening
Of my soul.
The white blossom of the wild plum
Is a song to the sun.
The small grasses are seeding
And little beetles are scurrying around.
Leaves are growing,
Flowers are opening,
Dragon-flies and swallows and bees
Are flying in amongst the trees,
And my spring thoughts begin to flower
From out of winter's lone cold tower.

Rebirth

I am emerging from an ocean of grief.
From the sorrow of many deaths,
From the inevitability of tragedy,
From the losing of love,
From the terrible triumph of destruction,
I am seeing the living that is to believed,
The laughter that is to be laughed,
The joy that is to be enjoyed,
The loving that is to be accomplished.
I am learning at last
The tremendous triumph of life.

At Malcolm's House

The bush is silent as I lie
At ease.
I hear the sound of bells
Ringing in the breeze,
The distant surf,
The whisper of trees.
The harsh fast song of the city
Is far away
Across the hills and across the bay.
As I lie
On my bed, the quietness wells
Into my mind,
The inner tension melts away
And I unwind.

. . . .

The beach curves like a new moon
Into the distance.
The surf tumbles murmuring on the shore.
The falling night mutes the colours of sea and sand.
The sea mist touches my face
And in the evening silence
I hear the whole earth breathe.

The Buddha in the bush

There he sits
In peaceful contemplation,
Amidst the tall trees and scrub,
Quiet in his little shrine.
The bamboo sways across the path
And the setting sun points its golden fingers
Through the trees on the hillside.
He is far from the frantic city,
From the warring world.
There he sits
Bringing stillness into my raging heart.

Welwyn House
(for P.C.)

The old house is full of the shades of lives.
Past times hang on its wide verandahs.
The old boards are worn by long-gone feet.
The door handles rattle with many turnings.
The wooden walls look dustily into the green paddocks.
Old house you are doomed.
Your past is past
And you are decaying with memories.
Old house, sleep you last sleeping
In your lush paddocks
Then close your eyes forever.
I will pray for your soul, old house,
When you are gone.

Voices of the past

How books preserve the soul of the past!
There, written down,
Are my special voices swinging across the centuries,
Calling to me.
My friends of the past times
Are with me from day to day,
Speaking to me from other places
And far away,
Giving me courage to face my own today
As they faced theirs
In all their yesterdays.

A sad song for Walt Whitman

Sometimes I give up hope for the world.
So much violence and hate —
How can I be hopeful about its state?

My heart is heavy today
And everything is grey.
Man uses man as prey
And what can I do or say?
O Whitman, today
I have lost my optimism
And I cannot sing with you.
I am lamenting the lack of love
And the enmity of comrades.

Answers

Why do we need continual answers?
Why do we need experts and authorities?
Why do we have to assure ourselves
That everything is known?
We need someone to ask
And someone to advise
And someone to tell us what to do.
Why are we so afraid
To find a question to which there is no answer?
I think that we are more afraid than our ancestors
Who knew that they did not know
And were afraid.
Today we are afraid to know
That nobody really knows
The answers to our questions.

Anguish of the World

Tonight
I am surrounded by the anguish of the world.
It has been raining all day
And I feel that the skies are weeping for mankind –
Weeping for all the young men dead in war,
For all the women enslaved and defeated,
For all the dead children, gone before their time.
The skies are weeping for the folly of man,
For into the sky poured the smoke
From the chimneys of Auschwitz and Dachau,
Into the sky poured the smoke of Hiroshima and Nagasaki,
Into the sky fled the souls of all those destroyed.
I wonder that the sky does not weep every day and every night
For the senseless folly of mankind.

Lament for a twentieth century Jewish child

Little child scrabbling in the dust,
Playing with water
And laughing in the sun —
Hair shining.
Eyes shining.
Do you know what they will say to you,
Out there in the world,
As you grow up to man?
You will be the killer of Christ,
Slayer of the God-son,
Still the scapegoat after all these years
For those who will not look
At their own hands
For fear they see their guilt.

Modern Calvary

Reviled and ridiculed,
Starved and spat upon,
They walked their modern road to Calvary
In crowded cattle trucks
To concentration camps.
Their garments were rent
And taken by the Nazi soldiers,
And the crucifixion took place
In gas chambers and with machine guns.
And the sons and daughters of God cried out —
'My God, my God, why hast Thou forsaken us?'
As they yielded up their souls.
But there was no-one to anoint
Their starved and broken bodies,
No-one to watch for any possible resurrection
And few who wish to remember this modern crucifixion.

The chosen people

My people have walked
Through the centuries of curses and insults,
Through centuries of persecution and violence and hate —
Hate from those who preach of love
And violence from those who speak of peace.
What courage to have persisted for two thousand years.
What courage to have continued to create
When facing continual destruction.
What courage to have gone on believing
When even God seemed to have forgotten.
O you who are not Jewish,
Would you have chosen to be chosen
Under such circumstances?

Rabbi Joshua

Joshua, the miracle rabbi,
Walked through the holy land
Teaching the Torah,*
Healing his people
And preaching the word of the Lord.
The Sadducees feared his following of Pharisees
For he taught the living law.
And the Romans watched and waited,
For his Lord was not the Emperor of the Romans
And the Jews were a stiff-necked rebellious people.

And a strange thing came to pass in the city of David,
That this Rabbi Joshua
Was crucified by the Romans
And became Jesus, God of the Christians.
And his people became their enemies
To be hunted to the ends of the earth
For a crime that was not theirs.

O Rabbi Joshua,
How you would mourn for the deaths of your own people,
For the persecution inflicted in your name,
And how you would weep
For the love you preached,
That has not yet come to birth.

* *Torah: — the Law of God, according to the Jewish faith.*

Some Jewish thoughts on a folk mass
(For M.M.)

When I sat in your church tonight
I did not find a different God,
I did not find a different feeling.
People were praying and singing,
And people were worshipping.
I felt at home in your church.

What are these differences
That have caused so much suffering
To my people over the centuries?
Surely the time has come
That we can live together at last
As friends and neighbours
And not as enemies.

A song for the Sabbath
(For A.S.)

O come
Let us sing the Sabbath peace and calm
In a house filled with beauty

O come
Let us sing of Sabbath joy and hope
With my friends whom I love.

O come
Let us sing of Sabbath love
With ancient mead
Warming us with living yet to be.

O come
Let us hear a Sabbath song
From ancient lands and ancient times,
Singing a blessing over us tonight.

Poems

Poems like buds are born
Into my mind,
Flowing and flowering,
Words that I find.

Where do you come from,
Words in my head,
Words never thought before,
Words never said.

Where do you come from,
Poems of mine,
Singing and winging
And heady like wine?

A strange song for A.S.

The pale green woman from over the sea
Came often to visit me.
Half the world she had sailed over
After her demon lover.
And still she had to sail away
She used to say
As she sat behind her mask.
What was her task?
Her dream said go, her past said stay,
Her demon lover called her away.
O what will she do, so torn in twain?
Has all her dreaming been in vain?
The pale green woman from over the sea
Came often and often to visit me.

Song to the sea
(For A.S.)

I sat on the shore and I looked at the sea
That is taking my friend far away from me.
It is calm and blue in the setting sun
And the sounds of evening are just begun.

"Cradle my friend in your arms, O sea,
Carry her gently away from me.
Rock her awake and rock her asleep —
Give her your comfort if she should weep.
Sing to her softly the old sea song,
Magic and ancient and deep and long.
Keep my friend safe in your arms, O sea,
As you carry her far away from me."

A Mosman song*

O I went down to Memory Park
One cold and wintry day,
And all the past was bare and dark —
What could I do but stay?

I wept cold tears for the dead and gone,
For the lost and the led astray.
I closed my eyes and I stood alone
While my memories had their say.

Then I went down to the Magic Grove,
And the wild wind danced by.
It was full of sun and full of love
And full of joy was I.

O Magic Grove is a wondrous place,
With singing trees and flowers.
The tears were dried upon my face
And I laughed and wrote for hours.

* *Mosman is a harbourside suburb of Sydney, with a park called Memory
Park and a tiny street called Magic Grove.*

Sunday

I have a whole day
Stretching in front of me.
What shall I do with it?
Sit in the sun, read a book
Or cook?
I could write a play
Or go visiting
And spend my day talking.
I could sit and knit
Or do a bit
Of gardening.
There in front of me,
Is my day
To do with it what I will.
I can fill
It any way
I choose.
I have nothing to lose.
I could walk through the bush
Or watch a thrush.
I could watch an ant or a bee
Or think about me.
Who knows what it will be
Or what I will do
On this new day
Stretching its wings in front of me?

I have felt like a stranger

I have felt like a stranger
Most of my life,
Unimportant and unnoticed,
One of the crowd,
Someone who did not matter,
Someone they passed by,
Quiet and ordinary and shy.
But now I have found
The people who are my friends.
Now I can shout aloud
That I am no longer a stranger,
That I can be myself without danger.
My people are important to me
And I am important to them,
And I am crying because at last I am come home.

How strange to think

How strange to think
That I am me —
This being that I am, I am.
That through this me, I see,
I think, I am.
How strange
That that out there
Is part of me in here.
How strange
That that out there
Would not be there for me
If I were not.
How strange
If I were not,
Then that would not be here
For me.

A comment

(For Sir Humphrey Davy who said, after he had discovered and tried nitrous oxide, "The universe has no opposite.")

The universe has no opposite.
It is seen as it is seen
Within the eye and within the mind
As it has always been.
I, too, have no opposite.
I am as I am,
Without and within,
Before, now and perhaps tomorrow,
I am as I am.

The still centre

Let peace com into my heart —
Let it creep softly in
Quieting my busy mind.
Let me find
Where stillness can begin
Without and within.
Let me find
How to become apart
From tension and fear.
Let it start
Quietly drawing near.

How many times

How many times
Do we meet a person face to face
And soul to soul?
How many times
Can we meet another
And the two become one whole
Just for a while?
Bodies may meet bodies
Every day
And yet their occupants are far away.
But when soul reaches out to soul
And barriers are gone,
One is no longer ever alone.

Inside

Inside
I have a feeling of quiet ecstasy,
A sort of subdued bubbling
Of poems surging.
I need music playing
For my soul is dancing —
It is wide open
And I see
All creation creating
For me.

Tides Flow — 1972

Sound of rain

It has been raining for days and days,
Almost without stopping.
The green branches of the trees
Are bent with the weight of water
And are dripping silver drops
Into the soggy earth.
The house is dark with rain clouds
And the sound of rain is like pale music.
I sit at my old desk writing,
Listening to the distant thunder
Rolling around the sky,
Wishing that my words would fall
Like the prolific rain
Onto my parched and empty paper.

My mind is a boat

My mind is a boat
Afloat
On an endless sea.
Sometimes the weather is calm
And there is no cause for alarm.
But I never know
When the wind will blow
Or the storm will rise.
Who can tell what the weather will be?
All I can do is sail on
Ready for what may come,
The storm, or perhaps the sun.

When hope has left my heart

When hope has left my heart,
Who will sustain me?
I cannot count on my loved ones any more, —
They cannot sustain me.
I cannot count on the goodness of man
For evil doers are abroad,
And the warlike are making war,
And the beauty of every land
Is made desolate by the despoilers.
I am overwhelmed.
I am without hope.
A time of great crisis is at hand
And I have no faith any more.
I am all withered up inside
Like an old leaf.
Now that hope has left my heart
Who will sustain me?

Into the depths
(In memory of Charmian Clift)

Last week
I could have cast my life aside
Like an old shoe —
I could have ended my stay.
I cannot tell
How seas of hopelessness
Drowned my soul.
I could not speak
Of my wish for death.
I drew into myself
Like a snail into its shell
Wishing for an end.
I withdrew from those I love,
Not caring for them any more.
There was a devastation
In my inmost soul
And a terrible aloneness,
And I was smitten down
Into the depths of the abyss.

My healing

I sat in my desolation
Withdrawn from all around,
Feeling my life was a ruin, a failure.
I was empty inside
With the utter collapse of my being.
I did not care anymore
For living or dying.
I was alone
In my distress and desolation.
But as I sat sadly on the ground,
The sun reached out his hand to me
And touched my face.
And so my healing began.

The Everlasting Sea

As I sit by the mighty ocean
Before the tumult of the waves,
I beat my breast
And cry at my hurt,
And still the waves roar in.
So will it be when I am gone,
When all my hurt and grief
Has been forgotten
In the sea of time.
When I am lain to rest
The eternal surf
Will wash this sand
Just as it does this day.
O everlasting sea,
Wash out my grief and hurt
And make me whole again.

I have been bereft of beauty every hour,

I have been bereft of beauty every hour,
Empty like an empty glass,
And cold with separation.
But this morning
As I turned the corner,
Beauty suddenly burst into my heart —
The harbour, shining in the glory of the sun,
Two tiny ferries floating in a sea of gold,
And there I was, alive again,
And living in the world of loveliness
That I had lost.

Song for Mikis Theodorakis

(Written during his concert in Sydney, 19th March, 1972)

At last the caged eagle is free
And there he stands,
Swaying and beautiful,
Far from his own land.
How he sings of his people,
The one who was jailed.
His handcuffed hands are free
And dance with his music.
His soul is bursting forth
Like a storm, like the sun,
Like Apollo newly-risen.
His music tears at my heart
And twists its sinews.
The eagle is free who was once jailed
And soars to the sun
In a torment and in an ecstasy.

Strength

Inside, I am making myself strong.
I am weaving bands of steel
To bind my soul.
I am knitting stitches of suffering into my hands
To make them strong.
I am strengthening my mind
With the warp and weft
Of weariness and endurance.
I am binding my faith
With the bonds of psalms and songs
Of all who have suffered.
In time I will be tempered like fine steel
To bend but not to break.

A memory

When my son comes home late,
He sits on my bed
And tells me about his day.
Someday he will remember this
When I will be no more,
When I have had my say
And gone before.
Then I will not exist
As I am now.
This me will be a memory
Of his when I,
Who now am here alone,
Have gone into oblivion.

We are all scattered tonight, my family and I

We are all scattered tonight, my family and I,
Over different parts of this wide city.
This is the beginning of our scattering
To the many winds of life.
This is the time of my children's going
And of my knowing that they are alone at last.
I am rejoicing that I am free
But I lament the past so passed and gone.
I am mother to children no longer
But to a man and to a woman.
Scatter, my children, and be free
But come back occasionally and be with me.

Poem for a Parting
(For A.S.)

I am looking at you
So that I will remember your face
When you are gone.

I am listening to you
So that I will remember your voice
When you are gone.

I am being aware of you
So that I will remember how you feel
When you are gone.

I am busy saving you all up in my mind
Because I am afraid I might forget your face
If you are gone too long.

The Train Park Revisited

Here in this park I sit
And fifteen years have passed
Since I last visited it,
Since I sat here
To watch the trains go by,
And count the carriages,
Under a cloudless sky.
The children laughed and swung on swings,
The hours flew by on rushing wings.
Now I am returned again
With tears aplenty shed,
Both children having grown and fled—
Their father ten years gone and dead—
And here I sit alone and watch the trains go by
And cry.

2 a.m.

As I walked through the house in the dark,
In the middle of the night,
All the doors were open
And the empty rooms
Glowed dimly in the cool moonlight.
My children, who lived in these rooms,
Have grown and gone.
There is a silence in the night,
An emptiness in the house,
And a sadness in my heart
For the years that have passed.

Last night I had deep dreams

Last night I had deep dreams
Sweeping me down
Into the dark depths of my mind.
When I awoke, I had to climb slowly back
Up a long ladder of weariness,
Puzzling upon the dream before it disappeared
In the bright light of day.
Yet now, when I am full awake,
The dream is with me still,
Clouding the back of my mind
With its hidden thought.
Strange how sometimes, when sleep is deep,
The dream stays on haunting the day.

Frisky

My cat sits quietly looking at me
With large green eyes,
His tail curled around his black paws.
He is proud and beautiful
And waiting to be fed.
He nudges me, whom he loves,
And pushes my pen with his head,
And we talk together,
My cat and I.

War

War is a periodic madness
Born of fear.
War is a constant sadness
Always near.
War is continuous killing
Always right.
War is fought by the willing
Day and night.
War is a killer of men,
A maker of graves.
War comes again and again
In terrible waves.

Thoughts at a Conscientious Objection Case

I sit in the court
And watch this boy speak for his life.
Below him, a young policeman sleeps in boredom;
The issue is not important to him.
The magistrate listens and writes carefully.
Below him, the court typist types.
The legal men whisper and search through their papers,
And the fans fly round and round on the ceiling.
The boy clutches the witness box
And refuses to become a soldier.
Here, in this courtroom,
Life and death have become a process of law
To be argued back and forth.
Here, matters of conscience
Have become a process of law
And the human heart is forgotten altogether.

Lament for Glen
(Killed in a motor bike accident, aged 19)

The splendid youth is dead and is no more,
And who shall comfort those who are left?
Who shall comfort the mother who has lost her son?
Who shall comfort the sisters who have lost a brother?
Who shall comfort the friends who have lost a friend?
And who shall comfort the father?
There is no comfort for those who are grieving
For faith is not enough
To assuage the tearing wound of sudden death.
O let me not drown in the flood of grief
For all young men who died before their time
And for this one so newly dead.
O let me catch the raft of life again
And not be swept away
Into the darkest depths of grief and loss.

Nothing to Say

When he spoke of your death tonight,
Silently I cried to myself, "no, no, not again!"
My eyes were full of tears —
I could not speak
When he spoke of that day.
I could only listen and cry inside
And go away.
Tonight, even after nine years,
When he spoke of your dying
I could only cry.
There was nothing at all that I could say.

Night Song

I lie awake in the quiet night
In the silence,
Not knowing the time.
All is quiet and dark.
I hear my watch ticking busily
Beside my ear,
Ticking the seconds of my life away
While I lie wakeful
Listening as they go.

Thoughts on Death

Some day I will die.
This person that is me
Will experience no more,
No longer hear nor see.
And yet the trees will grow,
The world go round,
Rivers will flow.
But I, that egocentric me,
Will have gone by,
Will not exist.
This is a time I cannot comprehend,
My own end.

The Mystery of Death

The mystery of death
Is that it leaves the living living
Whilst he who is dead
Has left an empty shell,
Has gone to who knows where,
Has ended.
The strangeness of death
Is that it comes to all;
It lies in wait,
Early or late,
For you and for me.
The mystery of death
Cannot be undone, cannot be understood,
For when it comes
We are gone, we are fled.

Lament for the Lost Beauties of the English Language
(After reading the plays of Synge and O'Casey)

O where are all our yesterdays
And the lilting language
Of the tongues now silent?
The language of today is cold and precise,
Technical and unsubtle,
Fit for the time of things
And of the turning of persons into things.
O who has stolen the language of the soul?
Where have we lost the song of the spirit?
Alas, they have gone
With the dream of the old days,
Gone with the passing of old beliefs
So that now there is nothing to believe in,
No future to sing songs and sagas for,
And the past is best forgotten and destroyed.
O let me lament the language we have lost
In the cold comfort of this modern world.

Police Court

I sat in that police court
And watched the magistrate inscrutably listening.
I heard the prosecutor intimidating and manipulating.
I saw the witnesses frightened or angered,
And the defendants bewildered and hoping.
I saw all the victims enmeshed in the trap of the law,
Struggling like caught fish to escape from the net.
But they will not escape, not any of them,
Neither defendant nor policeman, lawyer nor witness,
For all are trapped equally.
But only the victims know they are trapped.
The rest are slowly strangled
Until their hearts are hard and dry like desert stones
And, though they go on living,
They are dead.

Is There Anybody There?

I have looked at the world for many years
And have always assumed
That someone was running things.
I thought that governments were in charge
Of what was going on,
Or that big business was.
Others have thought it was the Communists
Or the Catholics or the Jews.
I have always assumed that somebody knew
Were we were all going.
Now, I am suddenly realizing
There is no one in charge at all,
Neither governments nor big business,
Nor armies nor anyone else.
We are all frightened enough as it is,
Believing that someone, somewhere, is in charge.
How much more frightened we would be
If we knew that there is no one running it at all,
And that there is nobody
Who knows where we are all going.

On Revisiting my Childhood Home after Many Years

All of this house was part of my formation.
All of this place became the background of my growing
The garden where I played is all torn out,
The fruit trees gone, the grass all driven to dust
And cars park endlessly in straggly rows
Where flowers and vegetables used to grow.
But there the house stands as I remember it,
Its old verandah gone, its backdoor shut,
The laundry turned into a laboratory,
Its inside torn and changed from home
Into cold offices and waiting rooms.
I am the only one who can remember it
As once it was — the place where I belonged,
Where I sat lonely, reading books all day.
Today the poor old house is blind,
Pushed up against a wall so that it cannot see.
Ghosts of my childhood walk around with me
While strangers work in every room I knew.

Holiday

I lie in bed bathed in moonlight
In the small house
In the middle of the valley.
All around are the low, dark hills.
There is no wind and everything is silent.
The moon is pale yellow
And is not yet full.
The sky is wide and dark and full of stars
But low, near the hills, is a pale, thin cloud.
I lie in the moonlight and think on him,
Lying in jail this night,
Who will not see the sky or the moon
Or this shallow valley
For three long years,
And I am sad that he cannot rejoice
In the beauty and freedom of the night.

Night song II

I am awake in the dark night,
Lying in the still house
Where everyone else is asleep.
At last the rain has stopped
And the wind has dropped.
I lie in my bed and listen to the silence.
I am alone tonight
Who would have company
Through the long hours until the light.

Going Home

We are driving through the night
Across this sprawling city,
Through the empty streets,
Past the black windows of silent factories.
Acres and acres of houses
Covered in darkness,
Tens of thousands of sleeping heads
In rumpled beds
All unaware that my love and I
Are passing by.

Pollution

As I ran beside the beach,
The cold gale from the sea
Struck at my body and face.
Its icy hands slapped my cheeks
And my eyes watered.
The sea spray was damp
And the roaring waves
Broke wildly on the land.
But at my feet on the sand
Lay grey sludge from the sea
And on the wild, white surf
Spread yellow foam
From the far city.
And, as I ran, I was angry as the gale
At the ruin of my beach
And the soiling of the sea.

Tudibaring Beach

I lie on the sand,
The sun warm on my closed eyes,
The long, pale beach curving into the dark hills.
Every now and then the surf is quiet
As if pausing for breath,
And then it rumbles on
With the continuous sound of moving waters.
Thin streaks of cloud lie
In the pale blue sky,
And the feel of autumn is in the air.
The white gulls walk delicately
Beside the surf.
The breeze gently blows my hair
As I lie quietly in the sun
On the still sand.

Woodcarving

Out of this old driftwood
Is emerging a shape.
Out of this gnarled and twisted root
My knife is seeking out a form.
Chip and carve and scrape
And the spirit of the wood
Is found and freed,
Lovely to touch and lovely to see.

Clearing Dead Timber

The flames leapt orange and gold
Up the green hillside.
The stormclouds rolled dark
Across the sky and sea.
Thunder thundered loud.
The lightning lit the valley
And the grey rain fell wetly
As we worked on the hill.
I felt the rain soaking my clothes and hair
As I chopped at the dead tree,
And I rejoiced at the wild storm on my hill
And the rain soaking me.

Tides flow

I lie on the beach with my eyes closed.
The late afternoon sun warms me,
And the surf roars in continuously.
As I lie on the sand
I feel cradled in the arms of the earth,
Protected and safe,
As the great world turns in the sun
And the tides flow in and out.

Seasons of Love — 1975

Silver trail

In my room, at my desk, I sit and write poems.
Sometimes I write in the car or on the beach or with friends.
I have books and books of poems
Telling how I feel and what I see —
My own vision of life written for me.

Sometimes I feel like a satisfied snail
Making a little silver trail of poems
Everywhere I go and whatever I do.

When you are far from here

When you are far from here,
My arms ache for the curve of your back,
My hands ache for the softness of your face,
My body aches for yours close by my side,
My eyes ache for your bright eyes seeking mine,
And my soul seeks you out and keeps you near.

When you are close to me,
My arms follow the firm curve of your back,
My hands caress the special beauty of your face,
My body presses close and close to yours,
My eyes clasp yours, and both our turbulent souls are one.

Today, as we talked in the sun

Today, as we talked in the sun,
I was glad, having you close by,
Near enough to touch, but not touching,
Near enough to kiss, but not kissing,
Stretched out on the grass, contentedly.

But yesterday, touching was not enough,
Kissing was not enough,
Holding your body tight to mine was not enough —
For the thought of death was at my back,
The final future loss was by my side.

O mind, take hold of thoughts like these
And put them by,
And give me leave my love to please
With joy until I die.

Time

I have loved you barely sixteen weeks —
That is no time at all
To have kissed your lips and cheeks
And let all barriers fall.

I have loved you a hundred years
This past one hundred days,
With much passion and even tears,
And in many and beautiful ways.

I will love you an aeon more
Before this life is finished,
Before we leave this earthly shore
And bodies both have vanished.

A Gift

I ran over the long sandhill
To the edge of the calm ocean
To meet the incoming tide.
The blue breakers were curling white
And washing up the steep beach.
The icy winter foam
Sloshed around my feet
As they sank into the sodden sand.
I gathered up an offering of tiny shells
From the edge of the surf
And ran with cold feet
Over the sandhill to my love.

Lying in my bed

Lying in my bed
In the middle of the night,
I listen to the rain pouring down
And the wind hurling itself
Through the trees.
How glad I am
To be warm and sheltered
On this wild, wet night
And lying with my love.

Driving back from the bush in the beating rain

Driving back from the bush in the beating rain,
I think of my house waiting to welcome me
With warmth and food.
Its strong rooftree will protect me
From this wintry weather
And its thick walls will keep me safe.
Driving on past the windy trees,
The rain sliding across my car,
I think on my house filled with my books
And the many things that I love.
My animals are awaiting me
And the rain and the storm are as nothing
On my long journey home.

Caterpillar

Fat, green caterpillar,
I found you eating my mandarin tree
And picked you off, on your little branch,
To kill you.
But then I looked at you —
Your little brown face,
Your tiny white claspers clasping the twig,
Your body olive green and brown and fat,
So beautifully caterpillarish.
There you are,
Just being a caterpillar on my tree,
How can I destroy you?
You are so beautiful.

Some days when I get up

Some days when I get up
I am so full of energy
That I spend my day in busy activity.
I mow the large lawn, sweating in the sun,
Heaving the mower through the long grass
And under the bushes.
I dig and weed and cut the hedge.
In my black rubber boots I squelch in the compost heap,
Turning over new soil, pungent and full of wriggling worms
Disturbed from their cool dark tunnels.
My dog follows me in high excitement,
Nosing the new-turned earth,
Nipping at my gardening gloves and barking at the mower.
At last I am tired with my day of doing.
I wash and drink tea,
While my tired dog sleeps and dreams,
Her head on my feet.

An interim

I am in an interim, a between-times.
What I was is becoming what I will be
But have not yet become.
What I will be is unknown as yet.

Does the buried cicada know
How it will come from the dark earth,
Split its old shell
And struggle into the world of light and air,
Green and alive,
Unfold its wet, squashed wings
Into transparent, shining beauty
And fly into the trees?

My shell is breaking
But O what will I be
When I step out into the light and air
Alive and free?

Winter

The branches of my liquidambar
Are grey and wrinkled and bare.
They reach up into the pale winter air
And darken in the cold rain.
But look closely —
All along the branches are tiny shining buds,
Promise of green leaves in the spring sun.
I, too, have tiny buds, promise of spring
And a late flowering yet to come.

Spring

This morning
As I walked across the grass,
The cold dew wet my bare feet.
My hair was cold and wet
And hanging damp on my shoulders.
I sat in the spring sun
Anointed on head and feet
With the water of life,
Amidst the celebration of blossom
Flowering on my trees.

There have been storms out in the deep seas

There have been storms out in the deep seas
And the beach is covered with tossed-up shells.
Heaps of brown kelp have been torn up
And washed into this little cove.
Here the sea has a low internal rumble and swell
And fast strong waves where usually it is still.
Somewhere out there in the ocean, there are storms going on.
Down in my own deeps, storms and changes are happening,
But I am only aware as yet, of tiny tossed-up shells.

Journey into the Shadows

Somewhere I have a shiver of fear deep down
For my friend who is ill.
She has fallen into the depths of the dark abyss
And is frightened to the edge of her being.
She cries and cries and is afraid to be alone.
She clings to me for help in the dark night of her soul
And I support her as best I can.
I stand as a strength to which she can hold in her desperation,
But secretly, now and then, my heart quails.
I am afraid for her
For I, too, have fallen into the dark ocean of the psyche.
I fear for her
Even while knowing that she, too,
Will come from this dread journey renewed and strengthened.

Young Man Dead
(In memory of Terry McQuade)

It is a beautiful night, warm and still.
The city buildings are glowing like palaces
And people in cars,
Gay on their Friday night pleasure,
Drive about alive and well.
But the young man is cold in his coffin
And his family sit and grieve.
What can I say to them who are bereft so suddenly?
Who can give meaning to so cruel a loss?
The young man lies cold in his coffin
Whilst we who are left, weep and live on.

Anzac Day, 1972

There are fresh wreaths around the white cross
In the Garden of Remembrance,
Fresh wreaths for the generations of young men
Dead in war —
Wreaths for the young men of my mother's generation,
Killed on the beaches and in the trenches
In the war to end war.
Wreaths for the young men of my own generation,
My friends and lovers, my cousins and brothers,
Killed in the desert and in the jungle
For freedom and a new world.
And now a new generation is ripe for new slaughter,
My own son and the sons of my friends.

Lay fresh wreaths, if you will,
For those who have already gone,
But I will not countenance another generation of young men dead,
Sacrificed to the insatiable god of war.

"Their names will live forever."
(From any war memorial)

Who can remember the names of those long dead
Who fell at Thermopylae?
Who can remember those who fell at Culloden?
Who can remember the legionaries
Who fell for holy Rome and emperor?
Who can remember the hordes of Tamurlaine
Or the armies of the desert whose bones are blown as dust
Around houses where children play?
Who can remember any who fell in long-forgotten wars
For long-forgotten causes
Now sunk into the silence of history?

O lying monument,
Promising false immortality to those who have gone
And those who still believe in dreams of glory
Ending in death and forgetfulness.
O lying monument,
Your names are already forgotten by the dead,
By the living and by those as yet unborn.

**For kangaroos, baby seals, bison, wolves, horses and all
God's creatures whom I love.**

With what unutterable cruelty
Men have treated animals
Since they began to mould the world
To their heart's desire.
Bought and sold,
Bred and exterminated,
Used and abused,
Created for killing
And killed for pleasure and adornment —
Our brothers, the animals.
With what infinite faith
You continue to trust us,
Even with our hands still warm
With the blood of innocents,
To do our every wish
And be gathered for the slaughter.

Do not give me a guru

Do not give me a guru
To sit at the feet of.
Do not provide me with a prophet
To follow into the wilderness.
Do not send me a seer with secrets
To guide me to life everlasting.
I am not looking any more
For someone to tell me the way.
I have found, in my life, many answers,
None of which turned out to be The Answer.
I have chosen various messiahs to follow in my time,
But each of them turned out to be false.
Now I know that I must follow my own heart
Along my own path.
Now I know that there are no answers
But only questions,
And the whole joy and anguish of living.

Tears of all the World

Why am I so choked with grief, so full of tears?
I have had sadness enough these last few years;
It is surely done and past.
But inside I have an ocean of grief
Welling up from some deep depths
Below my memory,
Weighing me down with the accumulated tears of centuries.
I find it hard enough to cope with my own grief,
But without help
I could drown in the tears of the whole world.

Day's end

At the late end of the summer's day
We came down to the beach.
The sea was smooth and pale,
Pale as the whitening sky
And there was no horizon to be seen.
The last rays of the sun
Caught a family looking for sea things
In the far rock pools —
Red and green and purple and yellow —
They looked like bright sea flowers
Clambering over the brown rocks.
The silver water lapped gently round the bay
And the warm sand cooled in the evening air.
At last my riven soul was quiet as the sea
At the end of this day,
After these past weeks of storm.

Overwhelmed

When I feel overwhelmed by destruction,
Let me go down to the sea.
Let me sit by the immeasurable ocean
And watch the surf,
Beating in and running out all day and all night.
Let me sit by the sea
And have the bitter sea winds
Slap my cheeks with their cold, damp hands
Until I am sensible again.
Let me look at the sky at night
And let the stars tell me
Of limitless horizons and unknown universes
Until I am grown calm and strong once more.

Balmoral Beach

In the quiet bay the beach is empty of people.
The small boats at their moorings
Float still and empty on this weekday.
The water is calm
But tiny waves wash onto the sand with soft gurgles.
Two seagulls float whitely along the water
And then walk up the beach on their thin red legs.
The leaves of the huge dark fig trees
At the beach edge, shine in the sun.
I have fled my busy phone and house
For this quiet beach.
I take off my sandals
And dig my toes into the damp cool sand
And am alone at last.

Into the ocean gently rolling

Into the ocean gently rolling
My body floats and is pushed
By the deep, curling waves.
The water is cold on my skin
And sprays saltily into my eyes.
Let me float in this cool sea water
Washing around all the continents
And all the beaches of the world.
Let me float with all the floating things in the sea —
Let me swim with all the fishes of the deep —
Let me feel the salt energy of centuries of sea —
Let me take in the calm and storms of the sea —
Poseidon's whole domain be mine.
Let me take in the free swirl of the green surf
And the chill water caressing my skin.

In me I feel the centuries stir

In me I feel the centuries stir,
I feel the ages turn.
What unknown ancestors have given me what I have —
What unknown generations have gone into my making —
The whole history of man
Lies in my two hands and in my mind.
This body is the chalice of life
Passed down from unremembered time,
Through unknown men and women
Lost in long-forgotten graves,
And given as a gift to me.
What I am now has come from what they were,
And what they were is part of what I am.
I am much more than a woman of today:
I am large,
I contain centuries and multitudes.

Feast your eyes on the tops of the trees

Feast your eyes on the tops of the trees,
Drink in the dark greenness of the tall gums,
Walk on the firm ground with bare feet
And absorb the stuff of the earth into your bare soles.
Take branches into your hands,
Feel the leaves with your face
And take in the inner growing of the tree.
Lie close on the leaves of grass
And let them caress your body.
Take the hot sun into your soul
And let the whole sky sweep into your mind.
Give yourself back to the living earth
And the earth will give itself to you
In unmeasured and unbounded pleasure.

A Glass of Water

Here, in my hand,
I hold this glass of water,
Transparent and clear and cold.
It is as old as the earth.
This very water has been flowing in rivers and seas
For aeons past —
Dropping as rain,
Evaporating into clouds,
Every molecule going in the inevitable round,
Incorporating and separating,
Becoming absorbed in and being excreted out of,
Wetting and quenching and osmosing and soaking.
This captive water in my hand,
How many times has it been drunk in history's rolling years?
It may be these same drops
Were drunk by Socrates in his last draught.
It may have flowed from English Harald's side
On Hastings field.
It may perhaps have writ
Sad Shelley's burning words.
My mind cannot compass
The long story of this water;
It is too vast.
Here, let me drink this water down and become drunk
With the history of the whole earth.

Sunset, Cape First Point

All around me are the blue hills and the green hills
And the dark, stark headlands
Standing out in the blue Pacific.
The long curved beach is filled with golden surf.
The lake is such shining gold
My eyes can scarcely look at it.
Down in the valley
The little houses snuggle close among their trees.
High on my hill on the vast cape
I am alone in the setting sun.
O how my heart expands and sings
With the glory of the earth
And my own happiness.

Full Summer — 1977

Leaves and poems

I sit at my desk looking out the window.
My mind is empty of poetry,
Dry as old dust lying under a bed.
Outside I can see a myriad of leaves
Of all the trees surrounding me,
Banana, liquid amber, peach and mulberry,
Grey olive, Pussy willow and lemon-scented gum.
If only I were hung with poems
As the trees with leaves,
How happy I would be.

The Mirror

When I look in the mirror as I wash,
I see a familiar face,
Older than it used to be, but me.
How strange it is
To have been living all this time behind this face
Looking out of those dark eyes,
Talking with that definite mouth,
Laughing, smiling, frowning.
I, who live inside this face,
Am still surprised to see it looking out at me
From my own mirror as I wash.

Autumn Leaves

The autumn leaves lay in heaps under the trees
All along the street.
It was my pleasure to walk ankle-deep
Listening to the rustling
As I shuffled them with my feet,
Pushing them, kicking and crunching them
In the far dream of my childhood.
A small girl alone with her thoughts,
The world outside, unknown and waiting.

Now I walk through the autumn leaves
And pleasure at the sight, the sound, the feel;
I, who now have passed the half-way mark
And know the world,
No more a child, yet childlike still,
Shoofing up the leaves with my feet,
And awaiting the miracle of each day as it comes.

Digging in my garden

This morning
When I was digging in my garden
I turned over a bright blue marble
Buried in the damp black earth.
There it lay, a memory of my children's childhood,
Hidden away these fifteen years
And lying safe until I dug it up today.
I washed it clean and placed it on my desk
To keep in mind those happy years now gone.

Weekday at the Beach

The beach is full of tiny toddlers
Tottering around on their new-found legs,
Falling down and getting up again.
There are the youthful mothers
Carefully watching their young
By the edge of the sea.
I, who have no small children any more,
Have escaped from the hot city
Jammed with cars
And watch with love
These young mothers with their tiny ones
As I dive into the blue sea
Alone and free.

Sea things

The rocks were covered with tiny crabs
And little scuttling things lying under stones
That rushed away as I disturbed them.
What right had this giant human
To come thundering into their domain
On this quiet weekday in early spring?
Bad enough in the summer
To be invaded by multitudes of children
Collecting shells and sea things
Whenever the tide was out,
But too much to be spied upon and upset
By some hare-brained human
Collecting beach stones in the off-season.

Sea Time

I awake with the sound of the sea in my ears
And all day it is the constant background to all I do.
As I sit and eat,
I watch the long waves rolling onto the sand.
I lie in the sun on the beach
And then walk into the icy ocean
To be buffeted until I am warm and brisk.
All day I watch the changing face of the sea
And at night its lulling song
Sings me to sleep and mellow dreams.

Dolphins

This morning when we woke
There were dolphins playing about in our bay,
Leaping from the water,
Tumbling and splashing in the sun.
We had a miraculous pink dawn,
Then dolphins off our beach.
What more could one ask for to begin a day?

The Dog and the Butterfly

Yesterday
A black dog chased a butterfly
All along the beach and back,
Leaping after it and running and doubling
Back and forth.
The tiny orange butterfly fluttered unconcernedly along
Out of reach
Up the beach and down again,
And finally off over the sandhills,
Leaving the dog panting and pleased with his game
And ready to sleep.

Empty Beach

There is no one at all on the beach this Monday morning;
The Sunday swimmers have dispersed,
The children have all gone to school,
The locals are busy with their own private tasks
And the long curved beach is empty.
There is only me and the sea
And the seaweedy sand and the sky.

Secret Place

On top of my cliff
We have a small secret place where we sit.
We have chopped down scrub and bush
To make a path to it;
Dug out the lantana,
Got scratched and twined in vines
Until we reached the top.
Here we can sit, alone and unobserved,
And no one at all knows where we are.
Here we can sit,
Surrounded by ti-tree and she-oaks,
And watch the ocean and the sky
And the incessant surf
Swinging up the curving beach.
Here we can sit
And let the city drain out of our bones
And be still.

Beach at Twilight

The sun has just set
As I sit alone close to the surf
On this long beach.
The surf is running heavy tonight,
Rough, foaming dumpers
Hurling themselves towards me
With thundering voices.
The pink clouds fade to grey
In the dying of the day.
I sit, taking in the never-ending energy of the water.
I think of the sea as the giver of life
And the taker of life;
It masters and dwarfs, cradles and plays,
Frightens and inspires.
I sit and bow my head
Before that great and ancient god, the sea.

Eyes

I have a pair of ugly eyes which I often use,
And out of them the sights that I see
Are hard and ugly and hateful and grey.
I see fear and I see lies —
I see killing and I see abuse —
I see blaming and I see misuse —
There is no mistaking the misery that I see.

I have a pair of beautiful eyes which I like to use.
And out of them the sights that I see
Are beautiful and lovely and true.
I see love and babies growing —
I see friendship and oceans flowing —
I see giving and I see creating —
And of the beauty of all there is no mistaking.

Today

Today
I have run away into crowded shops
And jostling thoroughfares
To escape from myself and the misery that is within me.
I have shut myself up behind my face
And moved to where nobody knows me,
Busily buying gifts and running away from my feelings.
Now, on this empty beach,
I can face myself and how I feel,
The paradox of knowing and not knowing,
The agony of loneliness within love,
And the entire contradiction which is me.

Prizes

I am caught up in the web of the world,
Its tricks, its lies, its pitfalls and its prizes.
I do not fear the tricks or the lies or even the pitfalls —
They are easy enough to see;
But its prizes might flatter and capture me.
It is the prizes that I fear
Because they shine so bright
And I half want their haunting light
To hang upon my hair.

The Bush

I have fled the dread city this morning
To the calm and wondrous bush.
I have fled from petty jealousy and the power hungry.
I have fled from the internal convoluted unhappiness
Of many marriages.
I have fled from corruption and hypocrisy and fear.
Around me are trees just being trees,
Not covering up their imperfections;
Around me are creeks, just flowing along,
Not tight and fenced in;
Around me are birds, just being birds,
Not puffing themselves up with their own importance.
All around me is the earth and its beauty
And I am freed from the toils of the city.

Un-Talk

What a lot of un-talk goes on —
Outpourings of words without meaning
Covering up an emptiness of heart and soul.
I am sick of long anecdotes
Told by people who have nothing to say.
They pour their emptiness over me
And would wipe me out with words.
With these people there is no exchange
So there is no real meeting.

Myths of the past

We have destroyed the myths of the past
So that we can be modern –
Scientific and not superstitious,
Rational and not magical,
Measuring to destroy the mystery
And denying everything but the usual.
We can admire the myths of the Greeks;
We can be condescending to the myths of the 'primitives';
We have given up the myths of our own religions
And have no meaning in our lives anymore.

I am making up my own myths for myself,
Knitting together old myths into new;
They are food for my soul
For I will die without beautiful dreams to live for.

Peace

I have left the turbulence of people behind
And entered into the calm of trees and plants.
My mind has been battered by other minds.
I have weaved amongst them, feeling them out,
Like a ship steering through cracking icebergs,
And I am tired with the effort.
Now I am surrounded by the souls of trees
And the broad quiet of the hills
And can let my tiredness go.

Christmas

Here on this empty beach
I have escaped from the hustle-bustle of mad Christmas,
Away from car-filled roads and anxious shoppers
And the whole hypocrisy of happy families
And holy family.
Here I can think of goodwill and love
And wish it more in evidence than it has been
In this century of war and the gas chamber.

Navy Exercise, Balmoral Beach

Seven black frogmen ran along the beach
Puffing and panting in the summer heat,
Toughened, roughened, hot young men
With hard, sharp feet.
Sweating in their rubbers
As they passed within my reach,
Seven black men of death
Running on my beach.

Night

Pull down your helmet of darkness
O night, over a tired world,
And let it sleep its dreams of dark destiny
Until the day returns.

Dreams of the unborn

What are the dreams of the unborn child
Floating so safely in its watery nest?
There, in the inside dark, eyeless and voiceless,
What does it see with the eyes of its mind?
Does it dream of the dawn of life,
The swish of salt water in the sun,
Sea creatures becoming land creatures,
Scales into fur and skin?

Floating silently in its private sea,
Does it remember other seas and other lives,
Other births in other times?
Does it dream of the storm to come,
The tumultuous tossing onto the shore,
The struggle to emerge to light, to air, to separateness,
To sight, to sound, to touch?
What, O what are the dreams of the small unborn
Before they join us in this milling world?

For Jeannie

Dear friend, you have accompanied me
Into the vast ocean of tears
Where my journey has led me,
Holding my hands as I wept.
Travelling alone is safe enough but lonely,
And I was pleased to have a companion
On such a cold, internal sea.
Dear friend, you have helped me weather my storm;
When you have wintry weather of your own,
Call me and I will accompany you
As long as you have need.

Secret answers

Down into the deeps of my mind I sink
To find the secret answers
I have hidden from myself over the years.
I am a little afraid of my own dark depths,
But I must search this unknown region
And make it mine.
It is a part of what I am
And I must find its hidden corners
And add them to the continent that is me.
Welcome, dark depths, light up your deeps,
Your creator is entering in.

Unseen world

Lying flat on the grass
I sink into a forest of green stalks and leaves,
Clover and seeds, moving in the breeze.
There are flies down here in the grass
And small beetles
And ants on long journeys
And little nameless jumping things.
The cool leaves of the grass
Touch my arms and face
And I smell damp earth and plants growing.
Down here in the grass
Is a whole world going on
That I never even notice
As I stride carelessly over it
Intent on my own important business.

Winter skies

The sky is especially blue this winter,
Flower blue, plate blue,
Pale and bright and beautiful.
The clouds, too, are especially cloudish today,
Great white bunchy clouds, almost pink in the sun,
Pale grey smears, windblown wisps,
Spread over the sky in whorls.
Strange that I have never noticed it in previous years
Or perhaps this is a particularly good winter for skies.

River Valley

Here is the total calm of the river valley
Under the midday sun.
All is silent and all is still.
The cows stand unmoving in the green paddock.
The birds are silent.
The river flats are moist and lush,
Sleeping the winter away.
The mountains loom darkly
On both sides of the river,
Ancient guardians of this old waterway.
There is no wind and even the grass lies undisturbed,
And I, in my car, am the only moving thing
In the entire valley.

Mountain Top

How beautiful is the dream of God.
On my mountain top
I am surrounded by mountains.
The birds are calling in the tall gums
And the little bush creatures are snuffling about
On their own business.
Down below there are tiny horses and cows
On the green river flats.
The river is calm and still,
And I see the enormous openness of the blue sky.
From my rock on my mountain top,
I see again how beautiful is the dream of God.

Night and the Moon

The moon is a sliver of silver
Curved behind a curtain of cloud.
Night has just fallen
And people are hurrying on their way home.
The little houses in my street are all lighted up,
Their doors and windows gleaming gold in the dark,
And smells of cooking are wafting about.
I, too, hurry along in the cold to my own warm house
And those waiting to welcome me.

In your Golden Light

I sit in the sun with my eyes closed
Soaking the warmth into my body and soul.
Same old sun that warmed Sappho as she wrote;
Same old sun that shone for Wordsworth and Whitman;
Same old sun, warming the blue-green world
As it slowly turns on its path,
Pouring life into all living things.
Poets have sung your praise since song began.
Poets will sing
As long as you hang brilliant in the sky
And the world turns, warm and glowing
In your golden light.

Such a lovely day of spring

Such a lovely day of spring
To sit in the garden talking and reading —
Stripping off clothes
To let the sun reach our white winter bodies
With warmth at last,
And dreams of summer coming.
Such a day of calm and quiet
With my friend and my animals,
Seeing pale plum blossom and pink japonica
And new green leaves and buds,
And feeling full summer and fruition on its way.

Wild sea

I sit and watch the wild sea roar onto the beach
With endless energy and hidden power.
Somewhere inside I feel the secret shudder
Of my own wild power,
Bound as yet but straining at the leash
To be unlocked, to be freed
Like the four winds from the heavenly places.

Will the wind never stop

Will the wind never stop,
Never stop its wild blowing?
Wilfully hurling the trees about,
Dashing along city streets
While people huddle against its swift cold arms.
Wind of the wild skies,
Why have you come to harry us, day after day,
And in the chill nights,
Rattling our windows,
Creeping under our doors,
Trying to reach us in our warm beds,
Whirling around our houses
While we sleep uneasily.
Wild wind from the high places,
Why are you plaguing us,
Throwing the rain against the walls
And the great waves against the cliffs?
O stormy South wind,
Fling your wild flurry against the hills
And leave us winter calm
To recover from your long unwelcome battering.

The Deep Wild River Hidden Below

At last I am tapping again
The deep wild river hidden below,
Shut away but roaring in my ears.
Who knows what divine madness
Will come from such freeing
And what fear and rough crossing,
But once launched on these magic waters
There is no safe return to dry land again.

Tomorrow's Words

Who can tell what I will be writing tomorrow?
Yesterday's thoughts are thrown away and forgotten.
The lines that I have already written
Lie darkly in notebooks in a closed drawer.
The lines yet to be written are waiting to appear
Out of the dark void where all words come from.
I shall wait quietly for tomorrow's words
To walk out of the shadows into my head.

Gifts and Remembrances — 1979

O, to be able all the time
To live a life of passion, poems and magic!

Gifts

I must be what people call a sentimental person.
I have worn my dead husband's watch these last sixteen years;
I use my mother's old sewing scissors,
Dull, grey, sharp scissors such as cannot be bought these days;
I wear my grandfather's old sovereign case
On a fine chain around my neck;
I remember playing with it as a tiny child
As I sat on his knee.
And from my father I have mulga bookends,
The only present from him I ever remember;
From my great aunt, a long, thin spoon
Which I measure out tea with;
From my grandmother, I have a strange, old, very useful tool,
Hammer, screw-driver and pliers combined;
And from one great grandmother whom I do not remember,
An engraved silver spoon,
Early symbol of my fortune in this life.

I love the continuity of all these things,
Knitting my past into my present,
Linking the living with the dead.
They have each left me a gift and a remembrance,
The completion of a circle which makes me whole
And strong to continue on.
I, too, will leave gifts and remembrances
For the continuation of those who will come after me.

Memories of my father

Throwing my mind back to my childhood,
I think of those now dead
Who people my past.
I think of my father,
Dead these forty years and more,
A silent, solid man
Who fled the Czar of all the Russias
To preserve his life and later, mine;
Who, quite unknowing, saved his whole family from war,
From the ghetto and the gas chamber.
All I remember is a quiet man,
Remote from children, not easily questioned,
Who died before I could ask him
All that I wanted to know.

For Muir, 20th December, 1976

Today, if you had lived,
You would have been fifty-six,
But it is only I who have reached it.
Sometimes after all these years,
I feel as if you never really existed.
Sometimes it seems like only yesterday
That we were young and full of years to come.
For seventeen years you were the companion of my body and my
      soul.
I have had lovers since, and friends,
But always I will remember you
With gladness and with sadness
On this the anniversary of your birth.

Destiny

Who could have known my destiny when I was born?
Just another girl-child to become wife and mother,
A vessel of life passing on life;
But here I am, having been wife and mother,
Promised to poetry,
Passing on not only children, but words into the future.
The muses must truly have blest my birth
And I, unknowing, came full circle into poetry.

For Po Chü I*
(Chinese poet, 772-846 A.D.)

For weeks now, on and off, I have been reading the poems of Po Chü
    I.
Well over a thousand years separate our lives.
Our times could not be more different,
Yet how alike our joys, our sorrows,
And how alike the problems of our lives:
To come to terms with power and government,
Both having been government servants;
To write poems everywhere we go;
To see others not caring for what we care for most;
To see futile wars and the capturing of territory;
To find friends of the heart to talk and feast with.
I am luckier than you, Po Chü I, who were exiled
And whose closest friends were exiled.
I live where I choose and have my dear friends near.

Dear Po Chü I,
I have read the poems in this year, 1976,
That you wrote far back and far away in the ninth century;
Which were, as you had hoped, preserved
And passed down the generations
Out of the cypress box you made for them.

Dear Po Chü I,
I would be satisfied if my poems lasted half as long as yours
And were half as loved,
And that some poet in five hundred years
Had as much joy from mine
As I have had from yours.

* *The poems of Po Chü I (白居易 or in pinyin Bai Juyi) were translated
    into English by Arthur Waley in his book, Chinese Poems, 1946.*

The Makers

Remember the tender hearts of those who make things;
Tread on tip toes around the souls of the creators.
Do not stamp with heavy boots
Lest each time they die a little inside.
A poet is like a timid phalanger
Gliding high in the tops of the trees,
She does not want to be netted or caged
Or brought down with a well-aimed review.
A maker must make as her soul directs;
A maker needs praise like God the maker
For while she is making, she is indeed God.

A Weight

Today I have a heaviness on me
And on all that I do.
Somewhere inside I have a weight anchoring me down.
I feel like an over-loaded ship in port
Tied to the solidity of the wharf.
I feel like a horse pulling a heavy dray,
Harnessed and blinkered between the shafts.
What weighty cloud must I throw off my mind
Before I can sail free again in the wind?

Lying on the long bush grass in the sun

Lying on the long bush grass in the sun,
I watch the slim she-oaks bending and swaying in the wind
And listen to its blustery whirring in all the trees on the hill.
Far below I can hear, too, the constant rumble of the sea.
Down here on the grass I am sheltered from the wind
But I can see the clouds being pursued across the sky.
The sun is my companion,
The earth is my place,
The grass and trees are my comfort,
The sea is my solace
On this especially alone morning of my life.

What is the matter with me?

What is the matter with me this beautiful day?
A pall of gloom lies over me.
Where has all my rejoicing gone,
My singing in the sun?
I am seized by thoughts of growing old and ill,
By thoughts of dying.
I, who am in the midst of life,
Am obsessed by death.

O let me grasp life with both hands
While I still have juice in my bones
And words pouring themselves into poems,
And the love of friends to sustain me!
Let cold, dark death withdraw
For I am not, as yet, finished with living.

Monologue for Henry Lawson*
(Written at the Henry Lawson statue, Sydney Domain)

Here I am
Standing alone in the rain below your statue, Henry Lawson,
On this grey, spring morning,
One live poet saluting one who is dead.
You and I are alone on this bleak hill
Whilst all the millions in this vast city
Are busy with their own concerns.

If you are up there, somewhere,
How you would smile to see this statue
Watching over a Sydney you would hardly recognise,
And which recognised you only at death with a grand funeral.
How you would laugh to see your face
On every ten dollar note in the whole land;
You, who had so little money in your life,
To be in purses and pockets and pay packets
In every home and every business.
Better my stories and poems than my face, you would say.

Lawson, my friend and fellow-poet,
You did it well.
You were never diverted from your path,
You never gave up.

Here I stand
On the wet grass below your statue,
Both of us soaked in the rain,
And accept your message this grey, solitary morning —
No matter what the weather of life,
No matter how stormy, how sad, how hopeless, how drab,
Never be diverted, never give up.

Lawson, you up there in bronze with your dog,
I salute you;
For your message and your strength on this grey day,
My thanks.

* *Henry Lawson's portrait was on all Australian ten dollar notes from 1966 to 1993. This poem was written in 1977.*

Silver Torch

Yesterday
I had my long hair cut off.
Suddenly, after all these years,
I had to have my head free,
My hair short, trimmed close to the bone
As I had it as girl and child.
From feeling old on my birthday
I now feel young and wild
And full of energy.
What is there about cutting hair off
That makes such a change?
For many years my hair was black,
Now it is a silver torch
Shining with years
And I am proud of its new splendour.

Let me fill my eyes with beauty

Let me fill my eyes with beauty every hour,
Feast them on the sea
And cows in green paddocks
And rain forests full of green rosellas and whipbirds and
          kookaburras,
And young bodies browning on beaches.
Let me fill my eyes with all the small grasses of the bush
And darting dragon-flies and tiny fishes and crabs,
And the stars at night and the moon.
Let me fill my eyes with beauty every hour
For they can never have enough of such loveliness.

Spring

Such a lovely spring of baby things;
Soft, brown-eyed calves
Nestling on the green hillside near their mothers;
Small magpies, their feathers all soft,
Running after their parents with open beaks
And all warbling together;
Pumpkin and passion-fruit vines running wild in the bush,
Heavy with pale, swelling fruits;
Little families lying on the beach,
Their small ones playing in the water.
I love the spring and the yearly renewal of life,
Eternal fulfilment of the promise of creation.

Four Poems

Today, already, I have written four poems.
Somehow I feel I should not write any more.
Four is a goodly store,
With that I should be satisfied.

Does the wattle say to itself
Only four gold flowers this spring?
Does the flowering gum say
Only four red blooms for me?

There is no limitation on flowering and blooming;
It is only I that am tied
To a smallness of my own making.

Beach Summer

What do people do
Who have no beaches nearby
And no hot summers of swimming and picnics?
Sydney people go off to the beach
As soon as spring begins to warm the winter ocean waters,
And all summer long lie on the beach
Or surf in the heavy waves of the Pacific
Until their skins are dark with salt and sun,
And sand scrunches on the floors of their houses
And has to be shaken out of beds and towels.
How do people live
Who never have the sheer delight
Of sea and sun at their doorsteps every summer?

The face of the sea

The face of the sea is ever changing;
All day and all night it changes with the tides,
Sweeping the beach clean
And messing it up again with seaweed and driftwood.
Smooth and calm and blue, it invites me into its cool waters.
Rough, with pounding breakers crashing like guns, dark and grey,
I am afraid of its anger and would not venture in.
At night, its blackness is darker than the blackness of the sky,
And it sings its old sea song to the earth and the stars,
Laving the lands of all the continents
With its cold, wet hands.
The face of the sea is ever changing and ever wondrous to me.

The Zen Dog of Tudibaring

There is a large white dog at our beach
Who stands for hours half in the lake or ocean pool
Watching tiny fishes or the shimmering waters
With concentrated intensity.
Now and again he barks at them
And then resumes his quiet contemplation.
I call him the Zen Dog of Tudibaring;
He is either old and wise or old and just a little mad.

Crabs

I sat on the damp rocks by the sea
Watching the small black crabs feeding,
Picking up their food with tiny, white claspers
And putting it into their mouths so delicately,
Like small children tasting a new and special treat.
They clung on to the rock as the waves broke over them
And, as the water drained away,
Went on quietly eating.
Seeing them like this, so small and so human,
I suddenly lost the unreasoning fear and disgust
I have always had for crabs.

New House

A house is being conceived on our cliff,
A house of sun and air, solitude and shelter,
A house of writing and contemplation
To be made manifest by architect and builder
Amongst the slim casuarinas.
Between the dream and the act,
Between the conception and the birth
Is the waiting and the growing
And the coming into being of what is being made.
A place of creation is being created on our cliff;
May many blessings fall on it.

Autumn Beach

It is still warm in the sun
On this late April day,
And the sea is calm and clear.
Winter is in the air
And the water is cooling from its summer heat.
We are the only swimmers now
As people begin to play football and hockey,
Knit sweaters against the winter cold,
And forget the existence of beaches until summer returns.
The beach is ours again this autumn,
Inviting in its emptiness and peace.

Driving

This morning,
On this beautiful autumn day,
I am driving my little car
Out of the city to the bush.
What pleasure to have an efficient and powerful vehicle
Under my hands and a long trip alone.
How well I understand the delight of man in the past
With a good horse under him
And a long ride to a desired destination.

Bush Honey

All over the bush the eucalypts are in bloom,
The branches laden with heavy creamy flowers
And humming with bees.
What a luscious harvest of honey
They will produce this spring,
Yellow box and peppermint and red river gum.

Winter

Most years I have not welcomed winter.
I have thought of it as a cold and stormy time
To be lived through until spring came around again:
A time to wear thick clothes
And sit in heated rooms
Or struggle through heavy wind and rain.
This year I am welcoming winter
And looking forward to the brisk cold
And the withdrawal into warm rooms to read and talk and write.
I am looking forward to the vigorous rain and storms
And the delight of the protection of my house.
This year I feel the strength of the winter,
A cold, dark time of the waiting of many seeds under the earth,
The cleansing rain;
A time of hot soup and toast,
And thick dressing gowns and slippers.
I am going to enjoy this winter
Instead of waiting, uncomfortable and complaining,
For spring to come.

European Civilization

Let me lament the triumph of the Europeans
Over all the peoples of the world.
Let me lament the triumph of white over black and brown and
    yellow.
Let me lament the tribes and peoples lost and destroyed
By invaders, exploiters and enslavers.
Let me lament the diseases spread and the cruelties inflicted.
Let me sing a song in memory of the ways of life destroyed,
Of the languages lost,
Of the religions ridiculed and crushed,
Of the ceremonies and customs abandoned,
Of the men and women and children
Driven from their lands,
Shot, poisoned, tortured, taken as slaves,
Forcibly converted, used and thrown away
With no further regard than rubbish.
Let me sing a song in memory of the lost tribes of my own land,
Whose blood stains wattle and eucalypt,
And whose bones lie scattered and forgotten,
Shards of their dreaming which we have destroyed.
Let me sing in memory of the tribes of the Americas,
Those that are gone
And those that are disappearing.
Let me sing in memory of the dark tribes of Africa
Who have lost the old ways for the new ways,
The factory and the mine instead of the hunt and the ceremony,
Humpies and degradation instead of the proud village,
The bull whip instead of freedom.
Let me lament again the triumph of greed and cruelty
And the superiority and rightness which justifies it all.
Let me lament for all these people, the simple and the untutored,
For their lives and their beauty which have been so wantonly
    sacrificed.

This poem was written in 1978, before the end of Apartheid in South Africa.

The Sacrifice of Trees and Animals

How many lives of trees have been extinguished
To make lamp-posts and houses, chairs and cupboards?
How many lives of animals have been extinguished
To make meat for the eating,
Fur for the wearing
And leather for the using?
And all without thanks,
Taken as a right and often with greed and for profit only.
They are taken without thought of the killing,
Without thought for the miracle of growth that has formed them,
Without blessing or thanks or even apology,
With no appreciation of their beauty in life
But only for their use when dead.
They are become mere commodities.
How long before we come full circle again
To first man's full reverence for living things?

The Old Men

Why do the old men destroy the young, generation after generation?
Are they avenging their own strength and potency now lost
By the killing of tens of thousands of beautiful young men?
Are they sacrificing their best to the gods
For the gift of life given to all?
Are the fathers wreaking their hatred on the sons
Who will replace them and make them seem as nothing?
The lies of the old men are preserved and perpetuated
By the deaths of the young.
Perhaps many deaths will turn lies into truth
In their twisted old minds.
I shake with horror at the continued destruction of young men,
At those who destroy and those who walk with open eyes to the
      slaughter.

The Voices of Women

Who will listen to the voice of women in the land?
The voices of men have the power and the glory;
The voices of men have the strength and the authority.
The voices of women are quiet and overwhelmed,
Not listened to and disagreed with.
The voices of men are loud with anger and cold with superiority.
The voices of women are full of tears and fearfulness
And trying to please but rarely pleasing.
How long, O Lord, how long,
Before the voice of women is listened to in the land?

Alien

Today, when I went swimming,
There was a tiny aboriginal boy
Playing naked on the beach.

Once this was the beach of his people;
Now it is the beach of my people.
Now he is an alien in his own country
And, on his own beach,
Appears an interloper amongst his white conquerors.

Paradox

Do not be trapped in doom or despair,
Do not be overwhelmed by misery and ugliness
For behind all lies the immensity of the universe,
The incontrovertible beauty and perfection
Of every act and counter act,
The inevitability of an end begun in the beginning,
The inevitability of a beginning begun out of an ending.
Out of the multitudes of the many
Is born the ultimate unity.
Out of the underlying unity
Are born the million, billion, trillion manys.
None are one and yet all are one.
Do not be trapped by despair
For out of despair many a new flowering may be born.

Healing

The task of the rescue of the soul is long and slow
And only those will be rescued who want to be rescued,
For only the soul itself can unmake
The prison it has so carefully constructed.
How delicate is the work of the freeing of the soul!
Open eyes and open heart,
A tongue to speak what must be said
And hands to hold through the terror and the pain.
Only those who are themselves becoming free
Can wield this fiery wand.
The rebirth of the soul is an agony and a joy
And only one already reborn
Can assist this painful labour.
How tender and beautiful is the work of the freeing of the soul.

Tears

I have a waste paper basket full of tears
Wept by my clients.
A pile of scrunched, wet tissues,
All that remains of sorrows present or past,
Flowing out at last,
Lightening the load.
They have brought their tears and left them here with me.
I can throw them out
Now that they have been shed
And their owners healed.

Differences

All the differences
And all the dividings
Must be suffered away
When the large work of uniting is going on.
All the sunderings must be put together;
All the misunderstandings must be understood;
All that has been unspoken must be spoken;
All the anger suppressed must be released;
All the grief that is left must be wept away;
All the hurt must be said so that the healing can happen;
All the fear must be felt so that the strength can come;
All the love must be loosed that has been hidden away;
Then the large work of uniting will be done.

Web of the world

In the whole web woven of the being of the world
Each of us has a place,
A small corner of the tapestry uniquely ours,
Spun in with our times and those around us.
We weave our own corner into its own shape
And all the tiny shapes become the whole,
And the whole moulds the little shapes
Until all are become part of one another.
No matter how small, all are required;
No matter how unimportant, all are necessary;
Each touches the whole and becomes a part of it.
Even you, even a small lizard, touches and changes
The skirts of the universe.

Remembrance

When I die
Will you be sad that I have gone,
Sad that our friendship has ended,
That our talking is over,
That we have parted?
Remember me.

When I die
Will you be glad that I lived,
Glad that we met,
Glad that we enjoyed so much?
Remember me.

When I die
I leave you love and the sea,
Friendship and all the loveliness of the world.
I bequeath to you, the living,
All joy and all sorrow.
Have courage always,
And sometimes, sometimes,
Remember me.

To You, The Living — 1981, 1991, 1992

I bequeath to you, the living,
All joy and all sorrow.
Have courage always,
And Sometimes, sometimes,
Remember me.

Bereavement and Loss

Your Death

The terrible devastation of the tearing apart
When you died so suddenly, so quickly—
There were no good-byes, I was not even with you.
You were gone by the time I came,
Soul flown from its earthly shell.
Yesterday a warm, living man, loving, caring,
Today a body, cold and abandoned—all life gone.
How could I believe you dead, you who were so alive,
My dearest companion for seventeen years.
Gone, gone, gone and I left to carry on.
How could I live with such a wound?
My soul torn apart, how could it ever heal?
What a devastation and grief entered my life
On the day you so unexpectedly ended yours.

After Seven Years

Seven years you have been dead
And it is like a lifetime.
Sometimes I wonder
If you ever really happened.
Sometimes it is only yesterday
And I know I will never again see your face
Asleep on the pillow beside me,
Never again see your head bent close over a book,
Never again hear your voice quietly talking—
And then I know
That I will always carry the scar
Of your sudden and too-early dying.

Dream

Last night
I dreamt my olden lover back from the grave
And in my arms again,
As if the years of death were but a dream.
He was as young as he was then,
But I was grey and older, as I am today.
I lay within his arms, comforted and comforting,
Forgetting in my dream that he was dead.
I had almost forgotten his gentle face
And the touch of his hands and his voice.

Anniversary

Today if you had lived,
You would have been fifty-six,
But it is only I who have reached it.
Sometimes, after all these years,
I feel as if you never existed.
Sometimes it seems only yesterday
That we were young and full of years to come.
For seventeen years you were the companion of my body and my
    soul.
I have had lovers since, and friends,
But always I will remember you
With gladness and with sadness
On this, the anniversary of your birth.

Memories

Today if you had lived,
You would have been fifty-nine
And grey like me.
It is nineteen years since you died
And you have faded to a memory at last.
I hardly even dream of you any more.
But yesterday I looked at photographs
Of all our time together, all our past,
Our friendship, marriage, children, friends.
How young we were there, side by side,
And innocent and full of life and fresh.
How beautiful we looked.
How far away and yet how near
Are all those years, the laughter and the tears.
How very fortunate I was
To find a loving soul like you
To live with for those few short years.

Funeral

Wattle and almond blossoms picked from home
For the tiny coffin of my grandchild.

Reminders

There are reminders of the dead child everywhere—
The cot, tossed and empty, that had become a deathbed—
Folded nappies awaiting tiny limbs now cold,
Shawls and clothes, carrying basket and pram.
There is the mother crying terrible tears,
Her breasts hard and aching,
Full of milk never to nurture the little one lost—
Her arms empty of the small, warm body,
Her heart irreparably torn.
There is the young father comforting the mother,
His own eyes red with grief,
His body taught with shock,
Holding the few photos and talking of his child,
The fact of death unreal as yet.
There are reminders of the dead child everywhere in this house.

End and Beginning

O you, who have returned to the infinite beginning
From whence we all have come,
Having made an end of what was begun many years ago,
Have you become a star in some undiscovered galaxy
Or are you a breath or a breeze
In the in-breathing and out-breathing of the universe?

For my Mother, Long After her Death

Forgive me, mother, for I have sinned.
I blamed you, in my blindness, for many things.
I held you off all my life, pushing you away,
Never allowing you near.
Only now I know how dear I must have been,
Though you could never say.
Only now do I see.
You gave me time and space and books,
Music, a room of my own and poetry.
You found me hard to understand
And I was intolerant with the sharp intolerance of youth,
Rejecting all that you valued.
Forgive me, mother, wherever you are,
For taking so many years to see
All that you did for me.

Collaroy Beach

Here I am, this sunny morning.
Sitting by the green winter ocean.
Watching the sun catch the breaking surf with gold,
Watching the darting gulls,
The black rubbered board-riders
Gracefully riding the waves,
The families picnicking on the grass
And wondering, wondering—
I have swum in the icy ocean pool
And sit warm and dressed in my car
In the midst of all this movement of water and people.
Pondering, pondering—
How is it that I sit here,
So strong and full of life,
When the husband of my friend,
Younger than I am,
Sits at home in a wheelchair slowly dying,
Having become an old man in a few months?
Sitting here, facing the continuity
Of the ocean, the beach and the sky,
I ponder on the living and the dying
That each one of us is here to do.

For my Cousin, Nancy

When I finally said goodbye
She cried hard sobs like a little child
And tears came to my eyes
For she is old and ill and vague,
But somewhere deep she felt we might not meet again.
She held my hands in hers, smoothing and patting them,
But could not speak
And I was choked with tears
Remembering the years between us and the love.
My heart was heavy as I went away
And left her in her room.

Importances

O how important are all the things of life,
Friends and possessions, political struggles
And the future of the human race,
Sex and sport and who said what about whom,
And the job and the shopping,
And being tired and being happy
And being young and being old.
How important all the everyday things are
Until death steps near
And strips away all the paraphernalia which surrounds us—
Then all these importances turn into trivia
In the face of the great mystery
Of where we come from
And where we go to at the end.

For my Old Dog, Tippy

When I stood there
And held your head in my hands,
I saw life fading from your old brown eyes.
Your head grew heavy as you slipped away,
Your eyes emptied and were still.
As I held you gently, stroking your soft fur,
I was sobbing inside.
My eyes were full of tears.
Silently I said goodbye,
Going away from the strangers who were there.
Leaving you with them,
I took my grief to have alone
Where I could not be seen.

For Frisky

I miss you, cat, since you have died.
I miss your pattering feet
Running down the hall when I come home.
I miss your loud demand for food.
I miss your warmth sitting on my lap
And your purr of happiness.
I miss our talks and you sitting on top of my books
After seventeen years, old cat, my house seems empty;
I miss your company now that you are dead.

My Dead

Today I have been thinking of all the dead in my life.
All my memories are stirred;
My private ghosts are rising
And my head is full of tears.
I had thought that they were all quietly bedded down
Deep in their old forgotten graves.
But no, my ghosts are risen in their full strength
And are walking round with me,
Pulling me back into far years and past events.
Lie down, my ghosts, and sleep.
Every day I have enough cause to weep
Without your clamour from the past.
Lie down and sleep at last.

Despair and Healing

Lost in Despair

Lately I have been letting my life
Fall into pieces about me.
All the old familiar ways have become meaningless.
I have been lost in despair's dark depths.
I have been lost in a forest of ills.
Wandering alone and calling for help,
I have looked to death as an escape
From the intolerable agony within.
Now it is time for me to turn from death
And chart another path.
Girding myself with courage and with hope,
I must find new tasks
And make a new beginning from an old and finished ending.

Courage

Call on courage when fear engulfs;
It is provided in limitless loads,
Enough and more than enough for all.
Never forget to call up courage in times of crisis,
In times of terrible loss—
It is the lifeline out of the abyss.
When all else fails,
Call courage to your aid.

Stormy Waters

What stormy waters have I been sailing through
These last few months!
I have not known whether I would come to port
Or founder on the way.
What storms of heart and soul have I endured,
Tossed here and there,
So often in despair,
I have abandoned hope for all so racked and tempest-torn.
And yet, battered and tired,
Uncertain, shaken but still whole,
I limp to port for shelter and repair.

Wiseman's Ferry

I first awoke
To the multitudinous cries of kookaburras
All along the wide river
Greeting first dawn.
I awoke again with the sun striking my eyes
From over the mountains,
Calling me to be up and out
To the lush bush,
To the tall white gums,
To the prawn boats
And the old graveyard.

The dew lay thick and wet
On the long grass among the graves,
And my dog bounded over them
Chasing butterflies and bees.
The old gravestones are tilting and sinking
Under the earth of the hill —
Old bones mouldering in old earth,
Making new earth and new life.
I could lie on such a quiet hill
By such a still, deep river
When my time comes,
And have dogs chase butterflies and bees
Over my discarded bones.

The Sixtieth Spring — 1982

I give to you, my readers, my poems.

I give to you, my readers, my poems.
All that I taste, I give to you,
All that I feel, I give to you.
Come with me, plunge into the cold ocean
And be rolled in the surf on to the shore.
Come with me into the surge of love,
Body with body merging and parting.
Come with me on to the factory bench,
Aching and tired beside others aching and tired.
Come, take my hand, little children,
Run into the years of manhood and womanhood,
Love and worry, disillusion and failure,
Success and broken dreams.
Come, take my comfort all those who are bereaved and lost,
Walk with me through the dark forest of grief—
I tell you that the sun still shines
And babies are being born.
Come with me, whoever you are, reading my words,
For my story is your story,
And our story is the story of every person there is.

Passover child*

How favoured by the stars was I at birth!
More favoured than I knew
For I was born on Pesach, a Seder child,
Born on the feast of freedom
Remembered by my people for three thousand years
In whatever lands they have found themselves;
And now, in my lifetime once more, in the land of Israel.
"Next year in Jerusalem" –
How many times in anguish
Have these words been cried out over the centuries,
From Babylon and Rome,
From York and Spain,
From Russia and Poland,
From the death camps and from the Soviets.
"Ma nishtanoh halailoh hazeh?"
"Why is this night different from all other nights?"
On this night we remember our slavery and our bitterness,
Our exodus and our freeing.
"Ma nishtanoh halailoh hazeh?"
"Why is this night different from all other nights?"
On this night I was born.
I remember my own personal enslavement,
My own walls of fear and sour aloneness.
I, too, have eaten herbs of bitterness
And shed salt tears for many years.
On this night I remember my own hard road to freedom,
The long unlocking of shackles
Until I, too, have reached my own land of milk and honey and
          poetry.
On this, my sixtieth birthday, and my sixty-first Pesach,
I give special thanks for my birth and my life,
My journey and my freeing.

* Pesach or Passover is the Jewish Festival which celebrates the Exodus of the Hebrews from slavery in Egypt. It is, therefore a feast of freedom. During the evening religious ceremony in the home, the Seder, it has been customary, for over two thousand years, to pray that the participants celebrate the festival "next year in Jerusalem".

My grandfather

I have four silver spoons won by my grandfather
In shooting competitions in 1903 and 1904.
My dear old bearded, religious grandfather
Who never in his life, to my knowledge,
Shot even a rabbit;
Who never went off to any war,
Though there were some on to go to at the time,
But spent his spare hours winning silver spoons
With his accurate rifle shooting.
I have these spoons and his old bible
And all my memories of this kind and gentle man
Who was such a crack shot in his ardent youth.

For my mother

You, who were my mother all those years ago,
I wish, O how I wish we had been friends.
I have just remembered that today is your birthday.
How I now wish that our differences could have been reconciled,
That I had been less wild,
That you had been less withheld,
That I had not fought you and disagreed.
You did not live to see any of your children's children.
Let me, who never thanked you in life,
Thank you on this, your birthday, for safely bearing me,
For nurturing me with food and books,
Music, comfort and security.
Mother of mine, I only wish
That I had said all this to you.
Instead, you are thirty years dead
And I, as old as you were when you died.

Mother and Child

I sit beside this woman
Who is racked with sobs for the loss of her babe,
My tears for her and her child dropping on to the table.
This woman is my child.
Twenty-seven years ago she lay cradled in my arms,
Nurtured and loved until she grew into childhood and womanhood.
Here we sit together, she cradled in my arms again,
And mourn the loss of her child,
Never ever to reach either childhood or womanhood.

For My Cousin Nancy

Last night I played Butterfly for you,
You, who used to sing it with such passion and power;
You, who had such zest, such humour, such energy.
I lament your living death,
Lying wizened in a hospital bed, sans mind, sans consciousness.
I weep for the loss of one who was dear to me,
One of the few I knew
Who took life into her arms as a lover.
Last night, my dearest coz,
I heard you voice as it used to be
And I wept, not for doomed Butterfly, but for you.

Spring

Spring is come again, the sixty-first of my life,
But my grandchild did not live to see even her first.

The Depression

When I was a child
Men walked the wallaby track looking for work
And were moved on from town to town as undesirables.
When I was a child
Women watched their hungry children grow thinner,
Patched their ragged clothes
And worried about their workless men.
Now I am past middle age
And the young workless crowd the shelters for homeless men.
Not allowed to move from place to place,
The young cower in their bedrooms
Or lie on the beach,
Filling in their days between dole cheques,
Or taking drugs to forget their uselessness
And the anger of those who work.
Fifty years separate these times
But it is the same old story.
How often, how often does history have to repeat itself
Before the lesson is learnt?

Disillusioned

I am alone on the beach.
It is cold even though the sun is shining.
I am feeling cynical and disillusioned.
The sea does not entrance me any more.
I am alone and out of touch
And feel squeezed dry by the past.
The seagulls are fighting and squabbling amongst themselves
And I do not believe in love any more.

I will feed my ears with music

How overwhelmed I can get by the bad news of the world;
Disasters in every quarter pouring into my ears and eyes
Until I begin to believe
In the coming of the end of the world.
I am sick of the talk of politics and power,
Manipulation and exploitation
And the inevitable doom of it all.
I will shut it all out of my head.
I will open my eyes to the sun and the sea,
To the dear love of my friends,
To the steady swing of the stars in the sky,
To the strength and bravery of ordinary folk living every day
I will feed my ears with music and poetry
And the voices of those who love me and whom I love,
With the voices of birds and the sound of the surf.
I will fill myself up with creation
So that the dark tide of destruction
Is not relevant to my life.

Winter Fears

It is dark and cold
And a bitter southerly is blowing the rain against my face
As I walk along the street.
It is the shortest day of the year
And night is drawing in early.
There are dissensions and strikes,
Unemployment and fear of the future
In my country this year.
In the winter of our lives
We forget the summers past
And the spring that will quicken our hearts.

Drag down the strong ones

Drag down the strong ones and the different ones
And crack their bones between your teeth.
Jokes and ridicule and contempt will keep them in line,
Or prizes and positions for those who can be seduced.
Let a thousand flowers bloom but cut down the tall poppies
For they endanger the whole crop.
Capture the creative ones and lock them in small cells of convention
Or debase them with subtle debasings that they do not even notice.
To step into freedom
Is to step into the danger of ensnarement
By all those who are imprisoned
And who are mortally afraid of those who are free.

When I am old and grey

On this winter holiday
We emerge from the house after the long rain
With all the other weekend holiday makers.
In the pale, warm sun we wander along the beach
Watching the cold surf tossing itself up the sand.
We walk on the soaked, green grass around the edge of the lake,
Under the tall, white paperbarks, behind the old lakeside houses.
I watch the reflection of sky and shore
And the breeze shimmering it out of focus.
When I am old and grey
I could live in one of these little houses by the lake
Instead of in our new fly-away tower house on top of the steep cliff.
Strange how I keep forgetting
That already I am grey and not at all young any more.

Aging

As I grow older
My teeth are beginning to chip and wear down.
I am beginning to feel like an old horse
Whose age can be gauged
By a quick look at its teeth.

Beach rock

The rock I am sitting on is warm in the sun.
It is very large and greenish-grey
And pitted all over with small holes.
Here it sits on the beach,
Rounded by the pounding of waves at high tide.
How many thousands of years older than me it must be.
It is full and curved like a pregnant woman
And not at all worried, as I am,
About how old it is and how many years it will last.

A Silver Hair

I found a silver hair on my blanket this morning
And I thought, who has been sleeping in my bed?
Then I remembered that my own hair is black as night no more,
But silver, like the moon, and it was mine.

Fifty-eight

I, who am now fifty-eight,
Well past, so they say, the prime of life,
Feel that I am only just reaching
The edge of my full strength.
All that has gone before has been a slow preparation
For the time of fullness approaching.
It has taken twenty years to clear up the clutter of a lifetime,
More to come through the wifing, the mothering and the widowing
To the healing and the writing and the time for myself.
Somewhere over the years, through the suffering and the satisfaction
And the whole tremendous experience,
I have found my strength and my confidence.
I, who am now fifty-eight,
Am looking forward with excitement and anticipation
To the next twenty years of my life.

City Pelicans

Today there are pelicans in the harbour at Pyrmont,
Calmly floating round the city wharves
Diving for fish between barges and tugs,
Bringing remembrance of lonely lakes and bush
Into the loud and busy city.

Night Drive

Night is coming to the mountains as we drive through them.
They darken as day fades.
The headlights of the cars are like gold jewels on the mountains.
The cold of the evening is setting in.
The wide waters of the Hawkesbury
Are steely grey and blue and black in the fading light
And soon it will be night.

Approaching Summer

Last week it was winter,
Icy winds and day-long drenching rain,
Heavy seas and the water like ice and rough.
Today the sun is warm with even a touch of summer heat.
The sea is tolerably cold
And I can stay in for more than a few frozen minutes.
On the beach, I can lie in a wet costume feeling warm
Instead of wrapping myself in a towel
And putting on my winter clothes at once.
Hail, approaching summer, I love your heat and long beach days.
I love your light cotton dresses and sandals and salads
And sudden southerly busters
And the caress of the warm sun on my darkening skin.

Beach Delight

Today the waves have washed piles of seaweed up onto the sand
And its strong smell is all over the beach.
Some small boat has been wrecked at sea
And all along the beach
We have salvaged useful pieces of timber washed up at high tide.
I float in a small, sandy pool as the tide comes in,
In turbulent water washing in over the rocks from the surf.
Why should I travel the world
When I can have such delight on my own beach
Day after blissful day?

My Dog

My dog sits on the beach, her head held high,
Her nose moving like a delicate antenna,
Catching every passing scent.
Her ears are tensed, turning to catch every sound.
Her eyes_are nearly closed
As she tunes in with nose and ears
To the multitudes of smells and sounds
That I am not even aware of.

I wrote a poem on the sand today;
The waves came in and washed the words away.

Alone

The lake is shimmering silver under the clouded sun.
The sound of the surf is like a loud wind.
The beach and the sandhills are empty except for me.
The trees are dark around the edge of the lake
As I lie on the sand, alone and content.

Butterfly and I

Here I am
Sitting in the sun on top of my cliff
Looking out over the Pacific,
Writing and listening to the waves
Breaking on the rocks far below.
There are three yachts in sight
And a low swell running.
I am well away from the edge of the cliff,
Sitting amongst the ti-tree bushes, westringia
And low casuarinas.
A brown butterfly flutters by me
And flies nonchalantly out over the edge of the cliff,
Unconcerned at the sheer drop
To the rocks and sea below.
How strange to think what different fears and confidences
We living creatures have.
I, who am so large and tall,
Am afraid to fall;
The butterfly, which is so light and small,
Has no concern at all.

How Precious is the Sea

The surf is fast today,
Big, curling dumpers throwing the board riders
Into the swirling white foam.
The sinking sun is silver on the sea
And the beach is misty with spray from the long waves.
How precious is the beach and the sea to me.
When I leave the city and reach our beach house,
I step from bustle and rush, into timelessness,
Into the infinite history of the ocean
And my own ancient roots in its watery depths.
I shed tight timetables and tension
And slip into days stretching out their hours
To twice their length
With peace and sun and trees.

Beach Walk

Down, down the long bush track to the beach we went,
Past the old sandstone cliffs and the great, rounded rocks,
Beside the pink, knotted apple gums and dark banksias,
Surrounded all the way by the delicious damp smell of the bush
To the empty beach.
Then back we came up the long haul,
Through the bracken and cycads,
And up the innumerable sandstone steps.
My two friends and I reached the top of the ridge
In a sudden fury of rain and wind off the sea.
Wet to the skin
We drove home for crumpets and talk and tea,
While the rain and the wind flung themselves
Around our little snug house.

Holiday

How delicious are dark bread and cheese,
Tomatoes and crisp onions
After a swim in the surging ocean.
Then a cup of tea and a quiet read
While I watch the great clouds rolling in over the valley.

Marooned

The thunder is roaring overhead,
The lightning is tearing the sky in half,
The rain is loud and so heavy
It has wiped out the whole valley around us
And we, in our house, are alone,
Marooned in the midst of the wild anger of the storm.

Writing Tower

Here I am at last sitting writing in our writing tower.
It is high here, overlooking the whole valley
And as high as the tops of the surrounding hills.
The sea is roaring continuously in the heavy southerly
And all the trees in the valley are bending and swaying in the gale
The beach is empty, the lake is grey
And the rain comes and goes.
I am alone in this little tower above the tree tops
In a world full of sky and poetry.

Wild Elements

Tonight the ocean is roaring at the foot of our cliff.
I hear it as I lie in bed trying to sleep.
The wind is loud in the trees
And is making the house tremble on its high poles.
I am afraid of the wild elements out there
With only the thin walls and windows
Of this fly-away house to protect me.

Wind

All day yesterday and most of the night
A wild easterly wind blew the rain against our house,
Bent the trees over in torrential gusts,
Rattled the windows,
Smashed our small hanging bells,
Blew the rain across the valley
Like white curtains shaking in the wind.
I could sleep only surfacely,
Uncomfortable in the continuous roar
Of the wind and the high seas outside.
I was in a restlessness because of the wind
And I felt at bay in our house
Whilst unknown battles took place all around.

Rainbow Lorikeets

In the morning and in the late afternoon
The rainbow lorikeets visit the trees around our house.
They swoop in and out of the she-oaks,
Feeding on the seeds
And crying out to one another.
They climb among the branches
And their brilliant red and green and blue and yellow feathers
Are almost invisible amongst the dark she-oak fronds.
They take no notice of me or my dog
But chatter as they eat,
Then swoop off with rainbow flashes across the valley.

Observed

Out of the blackness of the night
Flew a white, furry moth
Alighting on the outside of my window.
It shimmered its pale wings
As it looked with its tiny black eyes
In through the window at me.
How strange to be observed,
Like a large animal at the zoo,
By this small creature from out of the night.

Unconsciousness

How can people live as unconsciously as they do?
Listening and yet not hearing—
Looking and yet not seeing—
Eating and yet not tasting.
Living behind a wall of separation,
How can they go on being so deaf and so dumb
When the whole beautiful world out there
Is beating to come in?

The Beauty of Things

I can get drunk on the beauty of things—
Sunsets and the sky by night,
The colours of leaves, the taste of cheese,
The tints of earth and trees.
I can get drunk on the shimmering water of lakes,
The blue and green of the sea,
On a beautiful face,
On the shape of a shell,
In close talk with someone I know well.
I can get drunk on beauty almost any time I please.

Trollope's Reach, Hawkesbury River

The river is sparkling in the sun.
On the far side, in the distance,
The river's edge is a thin, silver strip.
The slender leaves on the tall, white gums
Hang still in the air.
Birds are calling and darting about.
The wide river is calm,
Creeping slowly towards the sea
Between the dark mountains on either side.
I sit in the sun
Taking in the stillness and the beauty
Which is here today,
Was present far back into the past
And will continue long after I have been laid in the clay,
And my adoring eyes are closed to all things beautiful at last.

Two Madnesses

I have been mad with poetry for years.
Now I am mad with drawing.
What two delicious madnesses to have
At this late stage of my life.

Stationery Shops

Do all writers get as obsessed as I do by stationery shops,
Which are full of blank paper, exercise books,
Diaries, fountain pens and ink,
Pencils and pencil Sharpeners and rubbers
And all the paraphernalia that writers use?
Stationery shops draw me with their magnetic power
And I rarely leave them without some new treasure
For my desk or study.

Let poems be born

Let poetry come sliding into my mind—
Let the lines flow in like a full creek.
Let me sink below the thoughts of every day
To where the dreams and poems lie.
Let them form like a child in the womb
Until they are ready to be born.
Let the words come that I seek,
Spinning into patterns of lines,
And let poems be born all the time.

Autumn Quietness

Autumn is on us after a long, hot summer.
The harbour is pale, white-misted in the sun.
Colours of shore and sea are muted, faded,
And a small, cool breeze is blowing off the water.
I sit on the sand contented with my life.
After storms and rough waters
I, too, have come to autumn quietness.
May it be a long and beautiful season for me.

Vocations

What strange occupations I have ended up in —
Psychotherapist and poet.
Who would have known, least of all myself,
That I would end up healing souls,
Holding in my hands the grief stricken, the pain-possessed,
The lost and the hopeless,
The ones who have lost their way
And the ones who have lost their feelings.
I came to poetry and to healing
In the fourth decade of my life —
The healing enabling me to become poet —
The poetry giving soul to the healing.
How unexpected and yet how right they both are.

Australia

I love the ancient oldness of this, my land,
With the marvellous stillness at its centre.
This land lies quiet and confident
In the slow wisdom of millennia quite beyond my comprehension.
This land is like a wise old woman, worn, knowing much,
And open as a book to those who can read her heart.
She will outlast us all.
We are such small, temporary dwellers
Within the compass of her arms.
She holds us for the moment of our life with love.
We pass and she remains.
I love this land where I was born
With a deep passion I have only just discovered.

After the bushfire

All the burnt trees are bursting out into a froth of new leaves.
The new bracken is carpeting the black ground.
Life is springing, like the phoenix,
Out of the fire and the ashes,
Creation out of the heat and the devastation.

The Sixtieth Spring

This is the sixtieth spring of my life.
My garden is full of flowers,
White may, orange nasturtiums,
Jasmine white and yellow, golden ochna,
And pink blossoms of crab apple and plum.
My garden is full of fruit, oranges and lemons,
Bananas and mandarins.
In this spring, too, the bush is full of wildflowers,
Great trees of yellow wattle,
White clematis, heath and bush mint,
And all the tiny flowers
Whose names I do not know.
I am sitting quietly in the sun
Trusting in many springs to come
Before I leave this wondrous and terrible world.
In this spring of my sixtieth year
My life is flowering and fruiting
Like the plants and the trees.
I did not expect such burgeoning
In these late years.

Below the Surface — 1982, 1990, 1994

Change

How easy it is for people to change their lives
And yet how hard.
We say—look what the world has done to me,
It is all their fault.
And we say—if only, if only—
We spend our whole lives making excuses and blaming others,
Creating and believing the grand illusion
That what happens to us has nothing to do with us.
How much harder it is
To see how we have very carefully made our lives
Exactly as they are,
That we are the authors of these messy tales
And we alone can change the story
If we will.

I have not understood

I have not understood what has been happening within me
These past two months.
Roaring oceans of grief have assailed me.
My world has fallen into tatters in my hands.
My past has risen like a dragon and swallowed me up,
Invading my present and twisting it up like crumpled paper.
I think I have been loosening my bonds,
Casting off from the past,
And out of what seemed to be terrible weakness,
Creating a new and magnificent strength.

How the past ties our hands

How the past ties our hands and ties our minds
Into tight closed patterns.
How much are our whole lives
Grooved into narrow moulds by the past;
Our emotions closed into little, shut cupboards
And the keys lost;
Our failures tied round our necks
Like old tins on a string
Rattling at all we do;
Our fears sitting on our shoulders like heavy packs
No matter how we run.
O let me break my chains!
Let my burdens go!
Let me find the key and be free!

Selected Poems 1963 — 1983

Scatter your words like seeds

Cast your words into the air —
Who knows who will catch their echo?
Cast your words into the fire —
Who knows what strength will be forged?
Scatter your words like seeds over the earth —
Who knows where they will grow?
Toss your words into the waters —
Who knows on what strange shore of the future
They will be found?

U.S.A. or Australia

My great grandparents, most accidentally, came to this country
Because they missed their ship to America.
How glad I am that they did.
What strange trick of fate or winds and tides
Tied up my destiny with this old south land
Long before even my grandparents were born.

Pyrmont

What a lovely morning of drawing in the sun —
Old, dilapidated terrace houses,
The wharves of Sydney,
Cranes and factories piled on the hills
One on top of the other,
And across the water, the city.
I sit on an abandoned block of land
Where once an old church stood,
And draw and draw,
And think on the hilly streets
And all the history surrounding me.
Generations of working people
Have lived around these wharves and factories.
I talk, as I draw, to one who was born
And has lived all her life in the same old house.
O I could spend the rest of my life
Drawing my beloved city
And never be finished with its beauty.

Beauty

Since I have been drawing
More beauty has come into my life.
Looking with an artist's eyes,
Not only the beautiful are beautiful,
But the old and the fat and the distorted,
All have their particular beauty of line and form
So lovely to draw.
Drawing has brought me even more beauty
Than I had thought possible.

Sitting in the sun

I ought to mow the lawn —
The grass is long after the rain.
I ought to clean the house —
It has not been done for a week.
My car needs cleaning and washing —
It is probably months since it was done.
I ought to make some phone calls —
I have been putting them off for days.
Instead, I am sitting in the sun writing poems.

Beach sketching

Whenever I sit and sketch on the beach,
Drawing people sunbaking or talking or reading,
They always move.
Invariably, by some unconscious awareness,
They know that my eyes are feeling their shapes
And putting them down on paper.
What unexplained sensitivities we must all have lying unused
For people to be so aware
Of someone they do not even know is there.

Paddington Market

In the shadow of the old church, the market sprawls,
Its many stalls crowded together in higgledy-piggledy lines.
Piles of floor mats and hats;
Rugs and shirts and skirts;
Every kind of shoe and pants;
Sandals and jewellery and rows of plants;
Clothes on hangers, old and new,
Drab or rainbowed in red and green and yellow and blue;
Things in baskets and sprawling on the ground.
The buyers and the sellers mingle and meet and talk;
Friends greet each other and walk
And the murmuring sound rises all around the church.
An old lady sits tiredly on a seat under a tree.
I try and catch all that I see
From where I perch and sketch.

Poet's way

I set out along the long beach, barefoot,
With a pack on my back,
And a green bamboo staff in my hand.
So must many a poet have set forth on his way
In centuries past, to find his dream:
So I set forth to find mine.
In my pack were my sandals, a coat,
And a notebook to write my poems in.
And I found on my journey some poems, a drawing
And a sunset fit indeed for a wandering poet.

Deep dreams

Let me sleep and let me dream deep dreams
Carrying me down to magic lands I do not know.
Let me go journeying all night
Within the mazes of my mind
Until day comes and the light.
Let me sweep out of the realms of everyday
Into the lands of faraway
Where griffins live and one can fly
And scenes of wonder pass the eye.
O let me sleep and let me find
Deep and miraculous dreams.

After my operation

Everything looks so beautiful to me
Now that I am on my way to recovery;
The pattern on my shirt,
My lunchtime grapes, so black; so round,
With a silvery bloom;
All the things in my bedroom,
The yellow rosebud, the pink chrysanthemum.
After a small encounter with death
The world is very beautiful to return to.

Convalescence

What a slow and lovely convalescence I am having.
I have nothing in particular to do.
I can stay in bed all day if I want.
I have piles of books to read,
Music to listen to,
Drawings to draw
And poems to write.
I can lie languidly in the sun
Or cosily in bed while it rains.
I have day after day being looked after
With meals and cups of tea, orange juice and salads.
I am being nurtured with tender loving care
And interesting conversations.
How could I help but recover
With such delightful treatment?

An ode to skin

Let me write an ode to skin
That covers us all over and holds us in.
It keeps our bones and flesh and nerves
And all our parts compact and in their place.
It covers our arms and legs and trunk and face.
It serves to separate us from everything around
And yet connect us by the way it feels.
How soft it is and firm and delicate;
How pliable, renewable and tough.
What amazing stuff, covering all our hollows and mounds,
So strokeable and often so out of bounds.
We brown it in the sun,
We cool it in the sea,
We wrap it, in the cold, to keep the heat within.
Whatever its colour, how beautiful is skin,
Pink or white, yellow or black or brown
Or any shade between.
It is the companion of all our years
From embryo until the end.
Let me praise skin which we use every day
And keep it clean and sweet
But never think of what it means.
This precious bag in which I live and use and grow,
My thanks for covering me from top to toe.

For my youngest brother

I little thought that you, the youngest of us,
Would be the first to go.
You seemed so solid, so respectable,
So certain, so unshakeable.
I was the rebel, the poet, the sensitive one,
Blown by the wild winds of emotion,
Following the hard road of the outsider,
And the eldest of us three.
Yet here I am, flying to Melbourne for your funeral,
You, whom I had always thought would surely outlive me.

Old life, new life

Spring is here, new green leaves,
Red gum tips, bottle brush blooming and fruit forming,
And an old man is dying.
New life is coming
And an old one is ending today.

My desk

In the corner of my study, under the window,
Is my old green desk that once belonged to my son.
Its drawers are full of writing paper and carbon,
Glue, ink, scribbling paper and folders
And all the other things a writer needs.
On my desk I have a small brass elephant
With a Bodhisattva on its back;
There they stand bringing me stillness and peace while I work.
I have an Indian box painted with bright flowers
In which I keep stamps.
I have a miscellaneous collection of pencils and pens,
Rubbers and pencil sharpeners
And sometimes my little green typewriter.
I have two smooth stones, one sandy-coloured and one black,
Which fit into my hands snugly and pleasingly.
I have a tiny box with a unicorn on it
And inside pebbles gathered by a friend from Keats' grave in Rome.
I have a lustrous blue paua shell from New Zealand
And a calendar above my desk
With a Hokusai print for every month.
I sit at my desk on my mother's chair,
Old and carved, with a tapestry cover that she made.
At this beloved desk of mine
I do my thinking and my working,
My dreaming and my writing.

Nails

Sitting in the sun in my garden on this autumn day,
I cut and file my nails and read.
I have cut my nails every month or two
For nearly sixty years.
From my birth until now
My ten fingers have been steadily growing nails.
My dear grandmother used to read fortunes in our fingernails
With some secret formula of her own,
Examining the spots and moons on each finger
And foretelling the future.
What did she see for me, her only granddaughter?
I have forgotten it all since those far off days;
She has been dead for nearly fifty years.
Did she foretell my destiny, my life of poetry?
I do not remember, yet here I sit.
Having become a grandmother myself,
And cut those same firm nails.

Hospital vignette

He was wheeled into the X-ray Department in a wheel chair;
He was dressed in an old suit without a tie;
He was well past middle age and grasped a thick walking stick;
In his buttonhole he wore an R.S.L. badge;
An old soldier, dozing as he waited lo be called,
And holding in his hand a large brown envelope labelled
FINAL REPORT.

The time for China

The time for China is drawing near.
At last, after all these years,
The fulfilment of my dream.
I will leave my own old land
To step onto the ancient soil of China.
From such sparseness to a country of such millions
Will be an amazement.
How strange, suddenly, to become so foreign.
I am frightened and excited at the same time.

Impressions of China

I have so many impressions to take in
That my mind is reeling.
All day in extreme heat
To the Summer Palace and the Temple of Heaven,
With tens of thousands of other people
Walking through temples and gateways, by lakes and palaces
Everywhere people and more people —
Curious eyes, friendly eyes, hostile eyes, cautious eyes
Of men and women and children.
There is so much to be taken in
That I am already full to the brim,
And we have hardly yet begun.

Beijing (Peking) I

All evening whole families sit on the pavements
And on the edge of the road,
Talking and fanning themselves;
Young men read under the street lights
Or play cards or talk;
Babies sleep in bamboo prams and children play.
The old men and women lie in deck chairs,
Fanning themselves in the heat
And no one worries what anyone else thinks
Of what they are doing
Or how they look.

Beijing (Peking) II

At what a slow pace this city runs.
Bicycles everywhere leisurely being ridden from here to there;
People strolling or squatting, talking on corners,
Or buying vegetables or icecreams;
Bicycles carrying desks or wardrobes,
And slow carts loaded with farm produce,
Small horses and slow buses.
No one hurrying, no fast traffic, no frenzy —
What a contrast to car-ridden, mad Sydney.

Xian

Today I have walked on the very earth
Trodden by Po Chü I,
The site of the T'ang emperors' palace.
Now it is a commune of twenty three thousand people
With farms and factories, schools and hospitals.
Everyone is well fed and well clothed.
Po Chü I would be pleased
To know that his people now own the emperors' land
And that they are neither poor nor beaten any more.

(Po Chü I: contemporary spelling, Bai Juyi)

The peasants of China

The peasants of China have continued for thousands of years.
They have worked and starved;
They have been drowned in floods;
They have fought wars;
They have had children, generation after generation;
They have been beaten and taxed;
They have praised their gods and their ancestors,
And they have gone on living.
They are still working in the fields,
Selling their produce,
Singing their songs,
Keeping away evil spirits.
They are the backbone of their country,
Starving no more
And with the green strength of the land
Still in their hands.

The light of China

The light of China is soft and pale,
The greens are green and lush,
Trees and rice and maize and mountains,
And the shadows are grey and soft.
In Australia the light is bright and sharp,
The colours are strong and even the greens are blue and red
And the shadows are black and deep.
In China I could not draw the curves of the roofs
Nor the curves of the bridges.
The little horses and carts
Trotted by too fast for me to capture them.
Even the street cleaners, old ladies with twig brooms,
I could not catch at their tasks.
What a maddening experience,
To be surrounded with pictures everywhere I looked
And to be unable to draw any of them.

The Entombed Warriors, Sydney*

Qin Shihuang Di, first emperor of all China,
Left his terracotta army guarding his tomb.
For over two thousand years, there they lay,
Buried under the earth,
Whilst wars and revolutions raged over their heads.
The peasants tilled the soil and lay beneath it
And the generations passed.
In the twentieth century, they were revealed at last.
I marvel at the dead hands that moulded these warriors;
At the many faces preserved for us
Whose bones are long since dust;
At the emperor who desired immortality
And the immortality that has been granted to him and to them.
I look with wonder at these warriors,
These men and their horses,
And I think of the passing of generations,
Of history, of families, of nations,
Of the anguish and joy of ordinary people.
As they have passed, so will we.
But we, too, will leave our own memorials
For future generations to find.

*Exhibition of some of the figures from the excavations near Xian, held in
  Sydney in 1983

China

China is on my mind and in my thoughts,
Weaving a web of fascination
So that I know I must return.
Somehow, despite my illness there,
My soul tied itself to that land and its people,
And my head is full of its colour, its buildings,
Its fields, its men and its women.
Now I have a new friendship
With two Chinese writers
And I must go back and see the country that they love
And all that I missed.
China drifts in and out of my mind
As I think of my friends
And my head is full of pictures of palaces and temples and tombs
And people walking in the streets
And working in the fields.
China has knocked on the door of my heart
And I have let her in.
I am drawn back to that immense and ancient place
Almost against my will.

Returned

I am lying down on the sand beside my special rock
Out of the wind and in the late afternoon sun.
After a week of rain and storms,
It is a great welcome to the sun I give.
After weeks of travelling in a foreign land,
It is with new and loving eyes
I see the surf rolling up my beach,
The deep ocean blue, the dark green headlands
And the sharp, open light of my own land.
How I longed for this, my own place,
When I was ill and far from home.
O rock, you have waited for me
And here I am, returned and in full strength,
To sit beside you and write by the sea.

Balmoral Beach

Grey, misty day,
Low clouds shrouding my city
Holding in the heat like a blanket.
The harbour water is almost white
Like a smooth, silver tray.
This morning the Navy is attacking my beach
And making a great noise about it.
I, who come to the beach for peace and quietness,
Have found only the roar
Of numerous landing craft playing at war.

High up on the heath

High up on the heath, I sit on white sand
And draw a clump of tiny bush plants,
Dwarf she-oaks and grasses and heath.
I forget everything —
There is only me and my pen and the bush.
Suddenly I am cold.
The sun is setting and my drawing is finished.
As I come down from the heath
Along the narrow path through the low scrub,
The whole ocean in front of me is pink
In the setting sun.
What sights to see — these tiny plants
And the splendour of the sea.

Our valley

This valley was once wild and full of trees,
With sand dunes and creeks
And the sea Wind rushing in over the beach.
Now it is becoming a suburb
With tidy roads and houses
And the trees chopped down for lawns.
All that remains of the past
Is the long beach and the wild wind
Rushing in over the sea.

Fishing

Here I am sitting on my pregnancy rock
In the last rays of the setting sun.
I, who now can only be pregnant with poems and drawings,
Have walked barefoot all along the beach
And found one small cowrie shell,
Some tiny shining ear shells, a wentletrap and some periwinkles
That I have collected in my pocket.
There is only one fisherman on this long curved beach,
And me, and I have already caught one poem.

Pregnancy rock: a large, rounded rock on Tudibaring Beach on which I
often sit to write.

Love will never go out of this world

Love will never go out of this world
For though hate and uncaring may seem to be triumphant,
Love is continually being reborn and discovered.
Love emerges suddenly in unexpected places.
Love renews itself continuously
Making meanings where there were none
And creating joy out of ordinariness.

My light

This month our valley is full of holiday makers
And at night the lights shine in all the houses
Like stars in the sky.
But when I stay up very late writing,
All the lights go out one by one
And the valley darkens and becomes quiet with sleep.
Then my light is the only one
Shining out from the dark hill.

Equinox, 1987

Who knows what message the morning brings?
Sea songs and seaweed, she-oaks and sunny days;
Grey clouds and grey gloom, dimness in an empty room;
Work and worry flying on quivering wings;
Who knows what songs the evening will sing?
Poems a-plenty, pleasing and full of praise.
Who knows the meaning of the dream of my life?
Least of all I, who can only speak of the beauty before my eyes

Womb of Words

Let me sink into the womb of words
Where poems are conceived and born
And where the deep secrets of love and life and death
Lie sleeping like undiscovered jewels.
O who knows what lost immortality
Will be found in these depths
Or what clouds of glory may be glimpsed
In the sudden moment of green surprise.

Childhood Dreaming

Who did I love in my childhood so far away across the years?
Was it my mother?
I was her first born, the awaited one and wanted.
It was never a comfortable relationship, I remember.
We did not understand one another.
She wanted me to conform but I always disappointed her.
Was it my father?
He was a silent man, old enough to be my grandfather,
Remote, immersed in his business.
I was only beginning to meet him when he died.
Was it my grandfather?
I was his favourite and favoured.
He was plump and comfortable and friendly
And bearded in a time when men were clean shaven.
He was religious and a good man
And more like a father than a grandfather.
Was it my quiet and lovely grandmother
Whose favourite was my next brother?
She totally accepted me.
She gave us puppies and kittens
And took us down to the wharves to buy fish
When the fishing boats came in;
She took us on picnics
And each month to visit the graves of her parents.
She, too, was a reader like me.
I loved them all in the fashion of a child;
They were the characters in the drama of my childhood
Until they began to die and, by my sixteenth year,
All were gone except my mother
And I was shocked forever out of the safety of my childhood
        dreaming.

Auntie Dollie

This morning I would like to celebrate my Auntie Dollie,
The sister of my grandmother,
Whose given name was Victoria.
She wanted to be a painter
But gave up this ambition to be a wife.
To the scandal of her family, she married out of her religion.
She had no children,
Lived a widow for many years,
And spent much of her time with my brothers and I,
Grandchildren of her beloved elder sister.
She lived in her small, old-fashioned cottage
Full of her own oil paintings
And cluttered with old furniture
And a grand piano that she never played.
She grew old, alone there,
Until one day she was found dead in her bed.
Dear Auntie Dollie,
I remember the expeditions we went on,
I, a small child, the laughing and the fun;
Having Sunday night tea at your house
And being walked home at dusk.
Once, when I was about five,
I lost one of dead Uncle Hughie's special horn tumblers in the sea
When it slipped out of my hand
And could not be found
After a picnic at the beach.
How upset we both were.
Dear Auntie Dollie,
You are one of the countless anonymous women
Who have lived and died uncelebrated,
Unremembered, unaccomplished.
Wherever you are, sleep deep and calm;
I will always remember what you gave me as a child.

My childhood

What do I remember of my childhood?
I remember a lonely little girl,
Living more in books than in her family,
In her own room at the top of the house
Where she could lie on her bed and devour novels.
I seemed far away from the everyday doings,
Far from the kitchen and the getting of meals,
Far from my small noisy brothers
And the comings and goings in the house.
I emerged every day to walk to school
And back to my private eyrie where the adventures happened,
Until I was called to tea.
I remember reading with a torch under the bedclothes
When I should have been asleep.
I wondered what I was supposed to be doing at school.
What a strange and serious little girl I must have been —
Stubborn, the family said,
Not letting anyone know how I felt.
Now, at sixty five, I am still strange and serious
But writing poems to tell the world how I feel.

Tonight I am playing old folk songs of the sixties and seventies,
The years when my children were young.
Days of the protest songs, of the Vietnam war,
Days of hope, days of dope,
Days of the dreams of a world of love.
And what have we got in 1984?
Days of doom and days of gloom,
Recession, depression and the young out of work,
Cynicism, corruption and dishonesty.
What has happened to the flower people?
They have grown old and conservative,
And the new generations are no less conservative
And shirk political issues for security of job and degree.
O we have lost our dreams
And live in the shadow of nuclear war.
Now my children have their children,
Born, as we all were, into a world we did not make.
O let their future be better than we can see —
For out of the doom, a new Phoenix may be born.

Lest We Forget

(For the three women gaoled for laying wreaths on the Cenotaph in memory of women raped in wars)

Let us not desecrate this War Memorial
With ideas other than those of sacrifice and bravery,
Queen and country, virtue and honour.
Do not remember and certainly do not mention
The women raped in war, in every war and by both sides.
Virtue is always on our side
And evil and wickedness on the enemy's.
In this man's game of violence,
Women are always the losers,
For not only are they raped
But their sons, their husbands, their fathers and their brothers
Are slaughtered as well.
Let us lock up these wicked women at once
Lest they diminish the glory of war.

My House

In my house, I have lived for twenty-seven years.
I have painted these walls and doors,
Scrubbed the floors,
Cooked and eaten thousands of meals.
I have lain in bed lonely through savage grief;
I have lain in arms, gazing with loving eyes
And body surrendering in the act of love.
These old rooms have witnessed much of the story of my life.
They have witnessed my despair, seen anger flare.
O I have tasted many loves beneath this roof,
Of husband, children, friends and animals;
And in this house was I, the poet, born,
Momentous rebirth into a world of words.
O wingèd Muse, choosing my house in which to rest,
You have brought blessing to a life bereft of song.
O home and haven, womb of my desire,
You have nurtured my inner fire
In the close cocoon of your rooms.
Much has been accomplished;
Tears have been wept,
Floors have been swept,
Someone has died
And I have grown more alive.
O house and home,
You have given a multitude of gifts to me.

Post Offices

I am glad that I live in the days of post offices
When letters that I write can be delivered
Anywhere that I send them.
How sad I find stories of the old Chinese
Who were exiled from family and friends
And could only send a letter
If they found a traveller going in the direction of home.
Perhaps it never even arrived
Nor would they ever hear from the ones who were dear.
Bai Juyi, the T'ang poet, going into exile,
Wrote a poem on the wall of an inn.
Much later, his friend, Yuan Zhen,
Staying in the same inn,
Found this poem and read with tears
The farewell message from his friend.

My Son

When my son came to visit this week,
We sat in the garden talking.
As I looked at him,
Suddenly I saw tiny wrinkles round his eyes
And a few grey hairs in his dark brown hair.
What a surprise!
How did this smooth-faced, curly-headed boy of mine
Turn into this tall man in his thirties
And showing the first signs of ageing
In so short a time?

Evanescence
(Written after the death of my youngest brother)

Tonight I feel the evanescence of life —
Now it is here and then it is gone —
Passed into the air like a piece of music,
Played and then heard no more.
All the solidity of everyday happenings,
The strength and beauty of people,
The weight of houses and buildings
And all the physical things that surround me,
Have become airy and insubstantial,
Made only of jostling particles of nothingness.
I feel as evanescent as a cloud, a leaf,
An insect or a wind —
Here and solid today, I, too, will be swept away
On one of the coming tomorrows.

Most of my life I have seen the world as full of mortality.
Now, as I am nearer to the end of my life,
I see the world as full of immortality.
How is it that it has taken me all these years to find this out?

Will I Be Reconciled?

I can never have enough of the beauties of this world.
Will I still be so besotted at seventy and eighty and ninety?
Will I, at the end, be reconciled to letting go
Colours and the sky, music, the sea and poetry
And all those people I have given my heart to?
O let me be able to part gently with the great feast of my life!

Lovers

This holiday weekend the beach is full of lovers.
There are also families and young people,
Grandparents and grandchildren,
But those I notice most are the lovers.
They hold hands;
They lie close together;
They are absorbed in one another
As if they are the only two people in existence.
O what a world of love and completion
Enfolds them and protects their every tenderness.

The Sea

What does the sea do to me?
It uncurls my soul;
It washes away my tensions;
It makes me whole.
The blessed sea holds me in its arms
Far from life's harms
And I, who am like a fish, come home.
O sea, never ever go too far away from me.

The language of the sea

What beautiful names some sea things have —
Glaucis glaucis, by-the-wind sailor, periwinkle and sunstar,
Wentle trap, sea dragons and many more.
The sea has a whole language of its own
Fascinating to those who love its ever-changing shores
And its blue deeps.

Dusk on the Beach

Dusk on the beach and the tide coming in;
The long blue dumpers crash up the sand.
The colours are muting and changing as I watch.
The sky and the sand and the sea
Fade into pale pink and pale blue
And there is a chill bite in the air.
I tramp home from the lake, my hands cold,
To hot tea and an evening of poetry.

Put uncertainty aside and let death slide out of mind.
Do not be blind to the possibility of an end
But do not let the spirit bend into despair.
Let it bear the future as a flower, delicately and with care,
With certainty and with flair.

273

Dying of Cancer

I cannot stand the agony of your dying.
I cannot even imagine what it must be like
To be trapped in a body racked with pain and desperate illness,
With no knowing how long the final escape will take.
It is not the death but the process of dying,
The agony that must be lived through with no one willing to shorten
      it,
And the watchers wringing their hands with helplessness.

Empty House

I must get used to coming home to an empty house,
To find no welcoming presence waiting for me,
No cosy lights and kettles boiling
For companionable cups of tea.
I loved coming home, knowing that you were there,
Working or writing and awaiting my return,
Both of us equally pleased to see one another.
Now I must become accustomed to coming home to an empty house.

Walking along this beach tonight,
I think of the many times
We have walked here together
Over the past twenty years
And my eyes fill with tears
Because you will never see it again
Nor ever walk along another beach with me.

It is so Hard to Remember

It is so hard to remember that you are dead.
At any moment you could walk into the house
Just as if you had been up the street shopping,
Or had just finished some writing.
Despite the fact that I walked with you
Every inch of the terrible path of your dying,
Sometimes, still, I cannot remember that you are dead.

Why has music gone out of my life these past few weeks?
I, who was nurtured on music since I was a child,
Could not have it playing at all.
I had to have silence, silence all round me.
What was I listening for
That my ears could not be diverted from?
Was I listening for a voice stilled forever?
Was I trying to hear melodies from some other sphere?
Was I hoping to hear the slow healing of my heart?
Was I catching poems floating in from some realm beyond this?
I needed silence for days,
But today I have found music again —
It has returned to comfort my silent soul.

Hang on to the rope of life —
Let it rescue you from the dark seas of death.
Hold on to the idea of living
Or you will be swept away
By the dark waves from the edge of doom.

You have gone beyond my ken to the starry places.
You are not bound to this world any more.
Never again will you be seen amongst the faces in the street.
Your friends mourn you;
Your mother's heart is sore.
Into what other dimension have you fled
Since you shed your earthly shell?

O you, who have returned to the infinite beginning
From whence we all have come,
Having made an end of what was begun many years ago,
Have you become a star in some undiscovered galaxy
Or are you a breath or a breeze
In the in-breathing and out-breathing of the universe?

Out of the Crashing Thunder

Out of the crashing thunder of the storm,
The cyclone at the centre battering my soul,
Cliffs of fall and I have fallen, frightful, sheer.
Comforter, where, where is your comforting?
O who am I, being wrought out of fire and tears,
Out of the wild sky and the dying,
Out of the tempest of my love?
Who am I, that am being tempered with fierce anguish and loss,
And making poems to comfort my poor heart?

This is a small new joy that I have found,
Lying on cushions on the floor in front of the heater
In pyjamas and warm dressing gown,
My animals basking in the heat,
While I read and write this quiet Sunday night.
From feeling alone and bereft, I am content.
Spring at last is on its way
After the most bitter winter of my life.

Lying on this beach in the winter sun,
I close my eyes and listen to the low murmur of the sea.
The continuous sound of the moving waters
Is soothing to the wounded heart.
I am sheltered from the wind
And the sun has a tiny touch of warmth;
It is gold on the slow waves
And I feel a small measure of contentment entering into my soul.

Alone

Today has been an alone day but not a lonely day.
I have spoken to two or three strangers and the garage man.
This morning I had a slow walk all along the beach and back;
I had four swims on the way in water so calm that there was no surf
      at all.
I sat in the shade of a cliff out of the sun
And sketched some rocks and the edge of the water.
I sat near the ocean and meditated
While the small waves lapped on the sand.
I let the day flow around me and I with it.
I came home to a piece of bun and tea and a sleep.
After lunch, I read and wrote and took my old dog for a walk,
And so the day has gone.
Now night is falling, the wind is rising
And I am pleased and fulfilled with all I have done.
Soon my friends will come and I will have talk to end my lovely day.

For Kiah

Farewell, dear old friend;
Go with my love to the heaven of dogs,
You, who have lived with me these last fifteen years,
Who have been my faithful companion,
Pattering beside me like my own shadow,
Sitting at my feet as I wrote,
Sleeping near me of an evening,
Walking behind me on the beach.
You had grown old and stiff and deaf,
But in this past year of my life
You have stood by me in my anguish and loss;
You have been my constant companion in my loneliness.
I will miss your scratching at the door in the morning,
Your excitement at a walk,
Your head on my knee when I was upset,
Your company in my car when I drove to our beach house,
Your enthusiastic welcome for my friends.
Go now, with my love, to the haven and heaven of dogs.

Rainbow Lorikeets

This morning a pair of rainbow lorikeets
Came to visit our house.
They perched together on the verandah rail
And peered in at us through the window.
I went out with food to welcome them
And they ate from my hand,
Chirruping and examining me.
Then the boldest hopped on my hand
And, walking up my arm,
Looked up at me and we talked
As if we had known each other for years.
What a wild and beautiful creature to converse with
On a rainy morning
Before driving back into the grey city.

Metamorphoses

From tiny egg to caterpillar,
From caterpillar to butterfly —
What mighty metamorphoses for such tiny beings.
How many great changes have I had in my life?
From seed to embryo,
From child to woman,
From woman to mother,
From scribbler into poet and artist.
And what of the internal changes?
From fear into confidence,
From anger into loving,
From busyness into calmness,
From sadness and loss into happiness and fulfilment.
How have they happened, these profound metamorphoses
That have wrought my soul into the person that I am?
How can I tell what I will be
When present storms have cleared
And changed my own internal weather?

Dream

I had a dream the other night of strange and beautiful ships
Sailing past me on a sea of calmest blue;
These old ships, such as I had never seen before,
Bright in the sunlight, lifted my heart anew
And stayed in my mind all day.
Their story hovered on my lips
But what it was, I could not say.

Precious Freight

I, in all my being, am woman and yet am not woman —
I am more than woman.
You, in all your being, are man and yet are not man —
Are more than man.
And you, child, are child and yet not only child but more than child,
Having the hidden adult within, growing like a seed.
Who are we all, we people?
We are all undoubtedly more than we think;
We are all undoubtedly more than we know;
We are also more beautiful than we realize
And more loved than we recognise.
We are full of hidden power,
Like deep racing engines running at half speed.
We have secret shadows that we dare not see.
Yet here we are, all of us, in millions and billions,
Living together on this earth,
Trying to work out our own destinies,
Trying to do our best — suffering, happy, anguished.
O little green-blue earth
Swinging out there in the infinite universe,
Spin safely with your precious freight of peoples
Round and round our golden sun.

The end of summer days

I love the end of summer days when the shadows are long
And the sun shines its specially golden light
On the glinting leaves of the gums
And on the seeds of the long bush grasses.
The breeze drops and the surf runs up the beach
In a froth of molten silver foam.
Little families pack up their beach things
And go home for tea and sleep.
I love the end of summer days
And the coolness of dark evening falling.

Bushfire

Black burned trees putting forth new leaves
In a pale green froth;
All around their trunks, blackened burnt soil
Greening with new grass and ferns.
Renewal after fire is the ancient story of this land.

The Great Symphony

Looking back down the centuries to the beginning,
If there ever was a beginning,
I hear the great symphony of man and womankind
Playing and replaying its many themes.
Each generation produces its own melodies,
Sees them as unique, as dramatic, as never expressed before,
And yet I hear the same themes, repeating and
        repeating —
The terrible marches of war and slaughter;
The lullabies of lovers and of mothers and the newly born;
The strong rhythms of the pioneers and the merchants and the
        builders;
The excitement and sadness of the young;
The disappointments of the old;
The rumble of natural disasters, of flood and famine, fire and
        earthquake;
And the low song of death, singing its slow counter-theme below
        them all,
Singing and singing.
Each movement is the same and each is different,
And the heart is broken and the heart is fulfilled,
And the babies become men and women and have their babies
And so it all goes on.
Loneliness and love, failure and success, loss and gain,
Pleasure and pain, again and again.
So it has been, so it is and so it will be,
The great symphony playing itself to itself,
Playing itself to us and to the universe,
Until the last syllable of recorded time,
Or playing, perhaps forever, because it is so true and so painful and
        so beautiful.

What is the measure of my time on earth?
Who knows, least of all myself?
What is the measure of the life I have lived?
No one can say until it is ended.
I have been born and I have grown;
I have been broken and I have been mended;
I have sown and I have harvested;
I have been young who now am old;
I have been shy but I have found confidence;
I, who was small, can now stand tall;
I, who was silent, can now speak out.
What is the measure of all I have done
And of what I have become?

Easter Equinox

Easter equinox, full moon, love, death and rebirth.
Eggs for the leaping of life, Phoenix born out of the tire and the
  ashes,
Comet across the sky and a feast of freedom.
The past falls away like scenery seen from a train.
Passion rises
And the future is being formed every moment under my hands.

Wild Winds of the Universe

When I opened my heart to love
All the wild winds of the universe
Took me in their arms
And shook the death out of my soul.

Fire in the Heart, 1990

Descendant of Migrants

My father and my great grandparents on my mother's side,
Came to this far country for its freedom
And its great distance from the pogroms of Russia and Poland.
"Let us go to the other side of the earth —
Sail into the south, into another hemisphere,
And there we will live as we wish
And have our children in safety and in openness."
It was a long and fearful journey
Across the oceans of the world in little ships
To a land they had never seen
But the omens were good and there was no going back to the old
        places.
From these momentous journeys I was born,
Both daughter and great granddaughter of these immigrants,
To put my roots down here.
To them it was a far country,
Needing a new language and a new way of life,
But for me it is my own country,
Rough and tough, with ways that I know
And a language that sings for me.
I do not know their old ways nor their old tongues,
Nor the dark foreign places from which they came,
But here, on my side of the world, I flourish;
Here, my children and their children flourish.
And what these ancestors gave me of their courage and their strength
Will never be wasted,
Nor will their love of freedom ever be forgotten.

Young Womanhood

O the days of my young womanhood,
How far away they seem
And yet how well I know
That shy dark girl who felt so unattractive,
Who did not know how to dress
Or how to talk in company.
She had a passion for poetry and wanted to be a writer.
She thought she was fat
But old photographs show that she was not.
She was avid for knowledge
And fought her mother for the right to go to university
Where she imagined she could learn to be a writer.
Her mother suspected that she would learn other,
Perhaps less desirable things,
And probably not return to the safety of the family nest,
And her mother was right.
She lost her religion, which was a great shock to her,
And then became a radical.
She went away on wicked weekends with the Labour Club
But did nothing more wicked than sing "Harry was a Bolshie" and
        "Joe Hill",
Went on long bush walks
And talked politics most of the night.
She found Bach and John Donne and Karl Marx,
Listened to discussions in the Caf
With young men who later became judges and doctors, artists and
        lawyers,
And young women who became scientists and doctors,
Teachers, historians and mothers.
She gave up her ambition to be a poet
Because she would never write as well as Shelley or Keats,
And threw herself with all her energies
Into politics and the war effort.

She did not, then, despite her mother's fears,
Get involved with men —
The ones she liked were not interested —
She was too shy and too reserved;
But she watched these young men going off to war,
Some to lie forever in desert sand or distant jungles.
I see her now as she was in those far-off days,
In her flat shoes and short rolled down socks,
Her plain brown skirt, tweed blazer
And her intense dark eyes,
Taking in everything that was going on around her,
Walking into a future that she could not see
With all the confidence of her youth.

Communism

In the thrill of youth
And in the sudden shock of losing my adolescent faith,
I came to communism —
The new faith for a new time,
A political instead of a religious religion
That would undoubtedly produce a golden age on earth.
At first I was a narrow and devoted devotee,
A true believer in this best of all possible systems.
I spoke on street corners;
I sold newspapers;
I went to innumerable meetings;
I pasted up illegal posters at midnight in dark streets
Full of zeal and excitement.
I must have been a slow learner.
It took me a long time for the flaws to become apparent,
For me to lose the blindness of total faith.
I kept my eyes shut and blocked my ears
And tried to keep my fairy tale dream,
But at last I saw the steel fist crushing the ideals,
The cruelty of blind fanaticism,
The calculating coldness of those in power,
Minds shackled and afraid,
Political leaders with the blood of innocents on their hands.
My illusions were shattered and that was the end of my communism;
I was cured of ever becoming a true believer again.
I think that a perfect system will never exist in this world
But I stand, as I always have,
For justice and freedom,
For compassion and peace,
For creation and the nurturing of the inner life.
Somehow, without any theories, humanity will muddle through as it
        always has,
And I leave it the poems of my muddled life

As some small comfort after 1 have gone.

My Diningroom Chairs

When I sit on my diningroom chairs to eat or to write,
I think of my beloved grandparents
Who, in 1888, bought them before they married.
These two young people, engaged and in love,
Handsome in the old sepia photographs I have of them,
Wandered around the Centennial Exhibition in Melbourne
And bought this set of elegant diningroom chairs
For their first home.
Who could have told the enraptured couple
That they would use these chairs for the whole of their married lives?
I remember their small dark living room
With the table and their chairs on one side
And my grandfather, sitting in his armchair with his earphones on,
Listening to the races.
I remember sitting on them for many meals
In the days of my childhood and growing up.
How surprised my dear grandparents would have been in 1888,
To have known that, in one hundred years' time,
Their only granddaughter and her grandchildren
Would still be using the chairs they bought that happy day.

My Mother

How can I write about my mother whom I really never knew?
We lived together for twenty-five years and yet we never fully met.
She was a strong woman
And I fought her for fear of being overwhelmed.
She was a conventional woman and I was a questioner.
She tried to mould me but I was stubbornly unmouldable.
She was religious and I became an atheist and then a Marxist.
We both loved music and the theatre
But I was a thinker and she was not.
She was secretly a generous woman, helping those in need;
I was selfish and self-centred with the intolerance of youth.
I could not reveal my heart to her
Nor could she reveal hers to me.
Even in her last illness we withheld ourselves from one another
And she died with nothing between us reconciled.
How can I write about this woman whose child I was,
But whom I did not know;
Whose outer life I could see
But whose inner life still remains a secret to me?

Motherless Child

Sometimes I feel motherless and fatherless in this strange world.
Here I am, alone in this confusing place,
In a changing time,
Trying to make sense of what is happening.
Is there anyone who can show me the way?
Who can one turn to, to forecast the future?
My only compass is my heart
To show me where to go,
But sometimes, when I feel like a motherless child,
I would like someone to take me by the hand
And guide me on my path.

Wet April

What is the matter with me this wet April?
Day after day the rain falls out of the sky
As if there is no end to the tons of water stored up there.
My garden is a lake, my garage is flooded
And the guttering overflows on to the soaking earth.
I am marooned in my dark house with a headache,
Full of a desperate aloneness that has crept up on me.
Oh April, April, month of sun and gentle autumn,
What has happened to you this year?
You, like me, have been overwhelmed
With torrents of tears raining out of the sky.
I know why I cry,
But why have you succumbed to such unexpected grief?

Courage

Call on courage when fear engulfs;
It is provided in limitless loads,
Enough and more than enough for all.
Never forget to call up courage in times of crisis,
In times of terrible loss —
It is the lifeline out of the abyss.
When all else fails,
Call courage to your aid.

Ghosts

Give up the ghosts of past love and past times —
Remove their remnants from the mind and heart.
They hang like pale scrim between me and my life.
Tear them down and scatter them away
So that I have the complete experience of now
Instead of old shades and dark corners.

Autumns

Autumns and autumns pile themselves up in my memory
And now another one is here.
Autumn — time of slowly putting on warm clothes,
Time of sunny days and cold nights,
And swimming in the clear warm sea.
The sky is fading from its deep summer blue
And the winds are rising to blow the falling leaves about.
I love each autumn as it comes
But I await with more eagerness
The spring that is coming.

The trees are stripped of summer leaves.
Their bare branches are held out like imploring arms in the pale sun.
I, too, have been stripped of leaves
And raise my bare arms to the sky and ask why.
I wait for an answer but there is none forthcoming
In this cold winter of my life.
I put all my faith in the spring,
The sap rising, the buds forming
And bursting into leaves and flowers and fruit,
And my arms no longer empty and imploring
But curved and full.

Winds of Change

The wind off the sea is whistling around the corners of this house
And I am upset by its whining.
It tunes in to some disturbance within me,
Some change a-coming,
Some fear, some inner quivering
That I do not understand.
O wind, you remind me of mountain blizzards,
Deserts' sandy blasts,
The honing of wind across prairies
And hot breath of the outback.
O winds of change,
Treat me gently as you pass through my life.

The gums are glowing green in the sun
And some are clustered over with creamy blossoms;
Their trunks and branches are white
And the wind waves their leaves about.
I cannot tell how I have turned from despair to hope,
From loss of love to the finding of love,
From emptiness into fullness.

Tidal Currents

My life is changing but what, O what is it changing into?
Deep tidal currents are washing through me,
Disconnections and connections,
Death wishes and life wishes,
Emptiness and fullness,
Busyness and quietness,
Uncertainty and faith,
All swinging me hither and thither
But nearer, on each tide, to the shores of life
And the richness of living.

Intimacy

How intimate is a plant with the soil;
Its roots, like many tiny fingers, spreading through the earth
Absorb moisture and food for its growth —
This intimacy is its life.
How afraid we mortals are of such a closeness —
Perhaps we will be swallowed up and lose ourselves,
Perhaps we will die.
We try to keep our separation at all costs,
Afraid and afraid.
O to be like a plant, unafraid,
Flourishing on closeness, being fruitful
And blossoming on intimacy.

Love

It is not just falling in love
But the weaving together of heart and soul,
The two separate lives joining into one;
The discovery of the body of the beloved and the pleasuring;
The talking and the exchange of pasts;
The day to day living and the shared future;
The magnetism that lies between;
The passion and the pain.
This is all love and the growing of love.

Love and Grief

How tied together are my loving and my grieving.
My loving has led to my grieving
And my grieving has led me again to love.
How can I untwine these two
Or is it the way love is,
Poised always between ecstasy and ultimate loss?

Wild Feelings

Sometimes I could burst with all the love that I contain;
Sometimes I could overflow with all the poems that are jostling
      inside;
Sometimes I cannot stretch wide enough to contain all the beauty
      that I see;
Sometimes I cannot bear to let all the sufferings of people enter into
      my heart.
Buffeted this way and that,
How can I learn to live with balance amongst all these wild feelings?

Who is to go?

How do we know who is to go,
Who is to leave this world
Suddenly, unexpectedly or in long pain?
There is no saying who will be with us tomorrow
Or who will be bowed in sorrow.
O, while you are here,
Grasp life with both hands
And pour your passion into living,
For who knows when you or yours
May be snatched away,
Out of the toil and the moil,
Out of our present existence.

Babies

Conceived in love or carelessly without intention,
We are all born into this world
To play a part in the drama of life.
Who knows what we will become,
What will happen to us,
Or how we will choose to accept
The gift that has been given to us?

Businessmen

The street is full of businessmen in dark suits,
Upright and uptight,
In black polished shoes and every hair in place,
Walking and talking of important things.
The buildings they inhabit are glass and concrete,
With automatic opening doors
And swift lifts taking them up to their computers
And their secretaries and their grey carpeted floors
And their fax machines.
This is where it is all happening —
Profits and deals and excitement and company lunches.
How can they explain to their wives and their children
That, if their hearts are anywhere,
It is there, in the market place, and not with them in their homes?

Day of Recognition

Mythical princes and princesses lost and found,
Hidden away like Arthur,
Until the magical day of revelation and recognition
When they discover who they really are.
I, as if I were in an old tale,
Thought I was an ordinary child, a commonplace girl,
A young woman like so many others.
My day of recognition came when I became a poet,
Joining the ranks of the truly blessed, the singers and the bards.
O, the beginning was hard,
Searching the labyrinths of the soul
To face Medusa and the dragons without sword or buckler,
With only truth and courage on my side,
And no going back once the journey was begun.
It is as the old tales said,
I have discovered myself not an ordinary woman,
Neither a princess nor a queen but a poet.

What are the tasks of the poets?

What are the tasks of the poets?
How to keep transparent like thin glass;
How to keep the heart open like a new rose;
How to tune in to the delicate nuances of others;
How to express the hidden words struggling to be heard;
How to live in an alien world and not be alienated;
How to contain the wild worlds within and not be split apart;
How to touch heaven with feet on the ground;
How to find a path in darkness and confusion;
How to make the lines sing and pluck the hearts of the hearers;
These are the tasks of the poets.
Do not envy them for their footsteps are covered in blood.

Creation

Creation is like a fire —
Once it is lit, it must be tended carefully,
It must be fed and kept burning
Through storms and wind and rain
As well as in times of good weather.
It can be extinguished only too easily
By desperation of the soul or by carelessness.
Then it must be lit again
And nurtured with the heart's blood,
For the artist must summon up courage and persistence
To be her constant companions,
To take her through the times of torment
To the clear flames of the full fire.

My Poems

Do not read what I write with the head but with the heart.
Read with the head, it is mere words skittering along the surface,
But read with the heart, it hits like hammer blows
On the deep bells of the emotions.
My words pluck the harp of the soul
With melodies unheard and hardly recognized,
To tunes of love and loss known only too well,
To visions unseen,
To beauty unnoticed.
Read my poems with the heart and the head
And they will sing their own songs especially for you.

Painters and Poets

Painters and poets are magic creatures,
Not quite of this world.
They come trailing clouds of glory,
Bringing their visions of beauty with them.
They are strange creatures,
Half mad or half wise,
And living in their own world of wondrous dreams.

307

Earth, Air, Fire and Water

The earth is spread out under me;
My feet walk its solid surface so lightly
It hardly feels my touch.
Earth is mother to trees and plants, animals and humankind,
Mother to the seas and all that are within them;
Its great consciousness wraps us all around
Though we do not know it.

Air is the breath and the breeze;
Air is blue and black in the sky;
Air is wind and oxygen in the blood;
It is flowing and still, heavy and light;
It wraps us round by day and by night
And we forget its essential presence.

Fire in the hearth and fire in the heart,
Destruction and creation, renewal and resurrection.
I live in it land that is renewed by fire,
That bathes in the heat of the sun.
We wrap ourselves in the warmth of fire
And we know its terrible power.

Water from the sky and water in the sea;
Water in our blood and in our tears;
Water bringing life to a parched earth;
Water washing us clean and running in pipes.
Play in water, drown in water, grow in water —
Water we must have and water we love.

Earth, air, fire and water!
Who would wish to alter these four essential elements of our lives?

Questions

Sand and salt water, sun and blue sky,
A faint breeze off the sea.
I lie on the sand
Watching the white clouds hanging high up in the air.
Why am I here?
Why are we all here on this spinning earth?
What fate is it that we all must share?
Heaven is so far and yet so near.
What is my life worth and what is yours?
Who can tell?
The surf rumbles quietly onto the beach.
To what depths and to what heights can we reach?

Stars

In the city the sky is smogged
And the stars pale in the reflected lights,
But up here, at my beach house,
The sky is studded with bright stars
Like a black velvet gown spread with jewels.
Here the sky is nearer to the earth
And I am nearer to the heavens.
If I reach out a hand
I could almost pick a star from the sky.

Beach House

I wonder, beach house of mine,
If you are lonely up there on your cliff
When you are left empty
And your occupants leave and return to the city?
Your doors are locked,
Your windows are closed,
Your blinds are pulled down,
Your power is turned off
And all is silent within
Except for the calls of the currawongs and the lorikeets
In the casuarinas that surround you.
What do you dream of in the silence?
Are you happy in your solitude,
Happy that those noisy talkative people,
With their meals and music and laughter, have left you?
Sometimes, in my city house,
I dream of you waiting for me to return
And, when I do come, I shed my city burdens
As I walk into your sunny rooms
To write and think and be.
I hope you are as happy as I am
When I arrive and enter into your sheltering arms.

Daddy-long-legs

At our beach house, while we are not there,
Tiny spiders and daddy-long-legs
Build little webs in corners and under tables.
When I come up each fortnight
I sweep them away and tidy up.
I suppose they think that every fifty years
Some terrifying giant appears, destroys their homes
And sweeps them out into the wild bush;
Then they slowly and carefully creep back again
And rebuild their webs
Hoping that the danger is over
And they will be safe again
For years and years.

Winter's Day

I am the only person by the sea this wild winter's day;
The grey surf is roaring up the sand;
The chilly gale is beating against me as I toil across the beach;
The seagulls are sheltering on the lagoon;
The rain sweeps in from the sea
As I turn up the dirt track to the road
And my little house on the cliff.

After my swim

After my swim,
I am reclining on the verandah of my beach house in the spring sun;
There is no wind and the dark she-oaks are still against the sky.
I have a fresh cup of tea to drink
And my writing and books beside me.
My feet are bare
And I have an old army hat on to shade my eyes.
I am alone with my thoughts,
Aware of the call of the whipbird,
The chirruping of the lorikeets
And hours ahead of me to do whatever I want.
What more could a writer ask for than this?

At Home

When I wake up in the middle of the night
My house is dark and silent.
Nowadays I live alone in the rooms where my family grew up.
All the street is sleeping at 2am in the morning
And it is too early for the chirping birds at dawn.
I am becoming used to the solitude
And feel at home in my house at night
When, not long ago, I would have cried
At the very aloneness in which I live.

Discovery

Strange how, for so many years,
My children were the centre of my living.
Now they are both parents
And have moved away into their own worlds.
I have had to learn to let them go and discover,
In this independent time of my life,
My own desires and loves.

Roads

When I was a child
I always thought roads were so permanent and solid,
Made by men with tar and heavy steam-rollers
For the passage of cars and trams, horses and carts.
Now that I am older,
I know that roads are just like silken ribbons
Laid on the surface of the deep layers of the earth,
Worn through in no time,
Washed away easily by rain and floods;
They are no more than long scratches made by tiny men
In their attempt to make the world into their heart's desire.
What I thought was permanent is impermanent;
What was made is unmade;
What was solid and real is swept away.
How like our own lives is the story of roads.

My Odyssey

My little journey into the country
Is nothing like that of Ulysses;
Unlike him, I know where I am going
And how long it will take;
Nor do I expect to meet any dangers.
But the internal journeys are another matter,
For I am both explorer and guide,
Facing the Cyclops, the Scylla and Carybdis of my own
And of those who come to me for help.
It is a dangerous and unknown world,
That of the mind, the emotions and the shadow,
And, like Ulysses' journey, the outcome is unknown;
Rough seas and possible shipwrecks can be anticipated
But with a pilot, a safe course can be charted
Through the dangers that lie in wait.
Courage is needed and persistence
To reach the haven where love is waiting.
Like Ulysses, I would not have the way safe
Nor the weather always calm
For the storms must be lived through
And the terrors of the underworld faced
Before the soul can discover itself and become whole.

Clouds

The clouds are low in the sky today,
Caressing the dark mountain tops
With their white damp hands.
There is no wind
And all the leaves of the trees hang still and quiet,
Resting until the next wind rises
To blow them wildly about
And to blow the clouds, like white sailing boats,
Across the sky.

Moment of sleeping

I turn my bedlamp off, curl myself up under the blanket,
Pulling my pillow around my shoulder
And let vague thoughts float through my mind.
I do not notice the moment of sleeping.
We never see the gate through which we pass
Into the lands where the dreams lie.
It is a mysterious journey that we take each night
As we abandon our consciousness,
And a strange return as we awake each morning.
Where have we been and how was the journey
That happens nightly to us all?

Beautiful World

What will happen to my beautiful world when my life is finished
And I leave it for some other place?
Will all the forests be destroyed?
The seas polluted?
The food contaminated?
Will there be nuclear war?
Will the greedy and powerful become greedier and more powerful?
Will despair prevail?
What will be the future of my grandchildren
And their children's children?
Pray that sanity will prevail
And this world will continue its existence in all its beauty.

Angels

I have not yet seen an angel
But I have found small signs of their presence —
A feather shed from rainbow wings lying in the bush;
A glint of light as the sun goes down;
An entranced face caught in passing
With eyes looking into another world;
A sudden glimpse of glory come out of nowhere
That makes my heart lurch.
Most of my life I did not believe in angels
But now I feel their presence everywhere.

How can we know

How can we know the consciousness of this planet?
Are we earthlings just tiny dots of life
Within the greater whole on which we live?
The moon pulls the tides and releases them;
The earth moves beneath our feet;
The sun bathes all living things in its light
And the wind and the weather swirl around us constantly.
How minute we are in the whole operation of the universe;
How huge are the oceans and the sky,
And yet we too, in our smallness,
Participate in the infinite process of the galaxy.

I tread the world lightly,
Hardly ever wearing out my shoes —
Not earthed too well, some might say.
Much of the time I walk as a stranger in a strange place,
Safely but aware of hidden danger,
Softly and on my toes.
Yet sometimes I walk as if I have inherited the universe;
I come as a queen with the sun on my face,
Tramping on the grass,
Shouting into the air because it is all mine
And it is all seen and it is all understood and loved.
I spin a web of words wherever I go
Which will endure long after these feet of mine
No longer tread the grass or the sand.
Then it will not matter
That I felt like a stranger or a queen
But only that I had been.

Journeys, 1992

Poets

In ancient China poets selected beautiful tools of trade
To place on their desks —
Special paper, brushes, inkstones, inksticks,
And pots to stand their brushes in.
Today, in these last years of the twentieth century,
I, a poet in the third quarter of my life,
Collect my own special tools of trade for my poems.
I keep my fountain pens in an inlaid wooden box;
I have my favourite sepia ink on my desk
And bound manuscript books
Which I keep in a carved oak chest in my study;
Bai Juyi, the Tang poet, in the ninth century,
Made a cypress chest to keep his poems in.
On my desk too, I have a collection of little figures
To help my words along.
Times have changed since the days of early China
But the habits of poets remain the same.

The Continents of the Mind

I have spent all these years exploring the continents of the mind
And still I cannot fully map their shores or their hidden hinterlands.
By some, their very existence is denied in sheer terror.
Some creep around their edges,
Not daring to enter the unknown terrain.
I walk safely through these landscapes
That are so familiar to me.
There are cliffs of fall, dreadful and treacherous,
And, at the bottom, the abyss, black and deep.
How to escape from such a place?
There are oceans of tears wept from innumerable eyes over the
        centuries —
How not to drown in such grief?
There are wild jungles of madness like endless mazes
And where is the hand to guide the lost?
There are quicksands of fear into which the unwary can slip
And who is to rescue them?
There are cold, cruel lands of ice which freeze the
        heart —
Erupting volcanoes of hot hate
And fogs of forgetfulness to wipe out the terrible past.
I walk in safety through these landscapes
And those who are desperate walk with me
Through these strange haunts
Into safe harbours and homely havens.
The continents of the mind change like clouds blown by the wind,
Never the same, never still,
And yet always known to me
As I guide the fearful ones out of the shadows
And into the sun.

Journeys

This weekend I have been to the mountains,
To the high rock cliffs
And the vast singing valleys of the Blue Mountains.
I have also been down into the depths of somewhere,
Past threatening chasms
To the great womb of the suffering
Of the lost mothers and the lost daughters
Of all the generations of humankind.
A healing was happening;
A daughter was being found and freed;
The ghostly mother was recognized
In her prison of terror
And plans were made for her release.
The outward journey is easy and a pleasure
But the internal journey is strange and unearthly
And full of dread,
Unreal and yet more real than real,
And the consequences none can foresee as yet.

Phoenix

Down in the depths of my being lies a phoenix imprisoned —
Imprisoned because I fear her power.
I pay occasional visits to this prisoner of mine,
Encouraging her, admiring her,
Telling her of the world outside,
Sometimes even taking her for short walks on a tight lead,
But I never let her fly.
Why, she might escape from her prison and from my control.
How would I cope with my passion and my strength let free?
So I keep my poor phoenix confined,
A beautiful bird locked in a cage.
When will I have the courage to let her free
And fly with her?

Houses of the Soul

Like Jung, I have a house of the soul to escape to,
To retire into the inner life,
Withdrawn for a little from the concerns of the world.
Jung's house had three towers,
Mine has only one;
His was built of stone,
Mine is made of much lighter materials
And perches, like a small Japanese temple, on its high cliff.
Jung built on the edge of a lake
In the middle of Europe;
I built on the edge of the Pacific Ocean
On the other side of the world.
Separated by time and space and generation
I, too, am following his path
But in my own way,
Towards the inner self and towards wholeness.

Summer Holiday

Sea and salt, sun and sunburn;
Meals and talk and the laughter of children;
Sand on the floor and sandals on the feet;
Summer heat, beach umbrellas
And the cold water of the ocean.
This is my summer holiday with my family.
What a week of fruit and bread and cheese
And young people's noise,
Reading and playing cards
And all falling into deep and satisfied sleep
At the end of each day.

Grandmothers

When I was a small child,
My grandmother seemed so old to me.
She was wrinkled and grey
And wore long dark clothes and large floppy hats.
Here, on this holiday with my grandchildren,
I am the one who is old and grey.
Living alone and quietly for so long,
The energy and noise of the young is a surprise
And I had forgotten their insatiable appetites.
How strange that I have lived years longer
Than my own dear grandmother
And that these descendants of mine
Will carry on the generations
Long after I have gone.
Then, I will be only a memory in their minds,
Just as now my own grandmother is to me.

Grey Storm

The grey storm is rising out of the sea,
Over the green headlands and the cliffs,
Chasing the sun out of the sky.
The crowds of holiday makers hurry for home
While the ocean darkens
And little thunders rumble around the clouds
As they approach the land.
I watch the storm with a heavy heart;
I cannot tell what dark gloom envelops me
As the rain begins to fall.

Music

I am listening to Vivaldi and Bach and Pachelbel
As I drive home from my beachhouse —
The same music that I played you as you lay dying
And moving slowly away from this world into the next.
It seemed the kind of music needed for the ending of a life
Just as it is the kind I need now for the calming of my life.

Contentment

The last of the sun shines gold on the lake;
It is sinking behind the black hills
As the ocean tide rises.
The sea is pale;
Long whisps of clouds lie in the sky
And the surf washes a thin mirror of Water
Over the high beach sand and into the lake.
The air is cooling with the approach of evening.
I sit on a sandhill watching men fishing
And children clustering around their mother.
My artist friend sits on the sand painting,
Catching the fading light.
At last, contentment is come upon me
After months of despondency and sadness.

On My Desk

On my desk, in my study,
I have a cluster of small figures
I have collected over the years.
I have two brass elephants —
One little fat one
And one, larger and solemn,
With a Bodhisattva on its back.
I have a bronze penguin, smooth and green,
And a carved wooden swan
Given to me by a grateful client.
I have a twisted piece of driftwood
That resembles a mother and a child
And a tiny piece of broken shell
I picked up on our beach
That has a strange horned creature attached to it.
And I have a bronze ram, copy of an ancient carving
That I bought for a few yuan
At the Great Wall of China,
Not even noticing, until I reached home,
That it was a ram and my Aries star sign.
All these things keep me company
As I sit thinking or writing at my desk
Or working with my clients.

Moonreader

Sometimes I leave my poems on my desk
After I have written them.
At 2 a.m., as I looked into my study,
My desk was covered in silver light.
The moon was reading my poems
As it passed by my house in the night.

Paper

I struggle daily with the rising tide of paper in this house —
Letters and circulars, booklets and bills, magazines and newspapers,
Leaflets advertising things I do not want,
Appeals for money and bank statements
Pour into the house in an unstoppable stream.
No matter how many I throw out, more piles accumulate
Until I fear I will end up buried
Under these growing mountains and mountains of paper.

Spirits

In old China, it was believed
That evil spirits could not go round corners
So that houses were designed with many corners
To keep the evil ones away.
My house has a straight hall from the front door to the back.
Chinese spirits would find entry easy
But I suspect that Australian bush spirits
Are not malevolent but curious
And like swishing through the front door
And out the back
To discover what is going on inside these strange boxes
That have been built in their land.

Southerly Buster

As soon as it came, I knew it was there.
From inside the shuttered house
I felt a flurry in the air.
From the heavy heat of the whole day
At last the cool wind had come,
Pushing the trees about, making them sway.
I opened the windows wide
And I opened the doors
To let the wild southerly buster blow inside.

Weather

Today is hot and cold, wet and dry, sunny and cloudy.
I do not think that the mistress of the weather
Can decide what to give us today.

Spring

Spring is almost upon us.
It is sunny and warm enough to take off my winter jumper.
The sea is blue
And in the bush the wildflowers are just beginning to open.
Why am I leaving my own beautiful land
To travel to far-off unknown places?

Paris I

What a strange thing, to be sure,
To be sitting in the sun in a park in Paris
Watching people on their way home from work or study.
The traffic is humming around the park
And children are running wildly about
Or walking sedately beside their mothers.
The sun sets late here and the twilight is long —
So different from the quick coming of darkness in my own land.
All day I have been roving around absorbing the city,
Taking its essence into my soul
Until I am full to the brim with its grandeur and vigour.
I am drawing its buildings
Until I know them with my eyes and my fingers.
Seven days is not a long time
To gather up memories like treasures
To be taken home and remembered for years to come.

Paris II

Every inch of this city is stained with blood
And throbbing with life.
It is steeped in history and covered in sculpture;
Statues of goddesses and muses,
Emperors and musicians,
Lawmakers, cherubs and horses
Sprout from old buildings.
It is full of eating and drinking,
Talking and laughing,
Lovemaking and tourists
And I, the poet, wander its streets
Absorbing all its nuances, its magnificence and its people.

"Forgive but never forget"
Written at the Memorial for the 200,000 French citizens deported to
concentration camps, Ile de la Cité, Paris.

Tears for the 200,000 French deported to the death camps;
Tears for the six million of my own people
Tern from their homes and sent to the camps of horror
And the gas chambers.
Tears for all those lost and destroyed,
For the families and homes broken and gone,
For whole communities eliminated;
Tears and anger for the sheer madness of wars and hate.
Yet here, after all these years, is the city that was defeated, enslaved
And is now at peace,
Its people strong and vigorous,
Its beauty preserved.
Forgive but never forget the senseless deaths and the slaughter.

Europe

History lies heavily here —
Times of peace and times of war,
Victories and defeats,
Depression and prosperity
And ordinary things like weddings and births
And tilling the soil.
Family sources go deep into the earth
And deep into the past.
In my country the roots are shallow as yet,
Hardly reaching much below the surface.
We are newcomers to an ancient land
Whose depths we do not fully understand.
No wonder we look with longing eyes
At these places that our families left.

Les Juifs*

My people lived in Europe for many generations
As despised aliens,
Persecuted by both rulers and the common people;
Forcibly isolated,
An exiled people who had no friendly home
Anywhere in the world.
I come now as a visitor to Europe
Years after the holocaust destroyed most of the Jews
Who lived on this continent.
Below the surface of everyday life
Still lie the seeds of the old hatred
For the descendants of their own god
Who hangs on crosses in every city and village I have visited.
I dare not speak of my origins here
For fear of arousing the sleeping hate
That still lies hidden in many hearts.

The Jews

History

History is the story of the rise and fall of civilizations;
It is wars and conquering,
Emperors and kings, luxury, prison, persecutions.
History is revolutions and tyranny,
Warlords and systems of law and politicians.
But how did the wives and mothers live?
How did the children live?
What did they do every day?
What dreams did they have?
Who did the cooking and who made the clothes?
Were they happy or were they sad?
Where is the history of the ordinary people?
Not the kings and queens or the lords and ladies,
Or the lawmakers or the lawbreakers.
We have made our histories into the stories we want to hear,
About important people and important events,
About heroes and about glory,
But we have forgotten all the common folk
Without whom there would be no history at all.

340

Noyers-sur-Serein

This little town sleeps in its history.
Its grey stone buildings and towers
Reach back into the centuries
Of dukedoms and marching armies
And walls to defend against conquerors.
The old moat has been filled in to make a road
And its cobbled streets are quiet
Under the tyres of visiting cars.
Everywhere I look there are pictures for me to draw —
Doorways, arches, lanes and roofs,
Old timbered buildings and towers and flowers.
I could spend months in this ancient town
Exploring and drawing its every corner.

Sydney

Suddenly this is my city —
Little old houses, terraces, brash new houses,
Tall glass buildings, wharves and ships
And the harbour —
All of it mine.
I come back after travelling the world
To find that my heart is here
And not in Europe.
There the people are immersed in tradition and the past —
Old hates, old fears, old prides.
I am for the new world here, where I live,
Where we are just putting down our roots
And building anew.

343

Returning Home

O the utter joy of climbing into my own bed, exhausted,
After weeks of hotel beds and travel
And trying to sleep on planes;
The joy of returning to all that is familiar
After the excitement of the unknown
That I have been taking in.
O, the cosiness of my slippers;
The taste of tea freshly brewed in my old brown teapot;
My house filled with my own things
And the garden run wild after the heavy winter rain.

Currawongs

The currawongs are having a meet in my garden this afternoon.
They are sweeping from tree to tree,
Calling out their melodious notes to each other.
Some matter of great moment in their bird life
Is being discussed at length
And no accord has been reached as yet.

Newspapers

Every morning my newspaper brings me
News of wars and slaughter,
Murders, crimes and injustice;
The rich becoming richer,
The poor becoming poorer
And corruption in high places.
I read the paper as I eat my breakfast.
Why do I continue to read such dread tidings
Before I start my day?

Cataclysms

What cataclysmic happenings are happening —
Earthquakes and cyclones;
Floods and storms and drought;
Weather all upside down and back to front;
Governments falling and new ones forming;
Old enemies reconciled
And old suppressed enmities rising and boiling;
Angers and fears, suppressions and freedom.
Underneath the outside eruptions
Must be an immense psychic disturbance on our planet
Or, perhaps, even in our galaxy.
Who knows where it will lead
Or what the ultimate outcome will be?

The Gnome

Sometimes, when we visit our country teahouse
For morning tea and cake,
We meet a gnome;
No bigger than a child is he,
With white hair and white beard,
Blue, blue eyes
And, when he smiles, only two white teeth.
Where has he come from,
This cheery messenger from another world?
He has never grown up, this little old gnome,
But he lightens us with his innocent smile.

Angels' Wings

The clouds are streaked across the sky
Like huge feathery angels' wings,
White against the blue.
Perhaps there is an angel up there
Flying so high that her cloudy wings
Are all that can be seen.

Tomorrows

Where have all my yesterdays gone?
My tomorrows are lining up to become yesterdays
And flow by so fast
That more than half a year has passed
Almost without my noticing it.
My todays pass like the turning over of the pages of a book
As they are read
Or like conversations after they are said.
I have had sixty eight years full of todays
Passing inexorably into yesterdays.
May be, at the most, I will have twenty five years of tomorrows.
Let them crawl by like slow careful caterpillars
Rather than galloping past like horses racing;
Then, perhaps, I can stretch out my remaining years
To twice their actual length.

The Hunted and the Hunter

For the past few months, and now that I am finally seventy,
I have been dogged by the idea of death.
It is following me like a hunter
Carefully tracking its prey.
I know it is there, not too near, not too far,
And there is no escape.
In my youth and in my middle age
I could ignore its relentless tread,
Pretending that it had nothing to do with me;
But now, at seventy,
I realize that the chase is nearly over.
I think I am not afraid of death
But of the process of dying —
Illness and pain,
The slow breakdown of the body
Or worse, the loss of mind and consciousness.
O hunter, when you finally sight me,
Shoot straight and to the heart.

Words and Meanings

The heart is in the hearth —
The hearth, the centre of the house —
The heart of the house.
Heart becomes hearth and hearth becomes heart
And in the centre lies art.
Fire in the hearth,
Fire in the heart
And fire in the art.
Place an ear on the breast
And hear the heart beating strong and loud;
Hear those talking around the hearth;
Hear the fire in the hearth burning and crackling
And warming those surrounding it.
All this is about loving and being loved —
About being warm and warming —
About hearing and being heard
And about making whatever it is
That needs to be made
Out of the hearth,
Out of the heart
And out of the art.

Winds of Change, 1995

Listen! Listen!

Listen, listen to what comes up from within.
Do not shut it out with busyness and activities
For the messages come from the great well of the unconscious
Where everything is known and nothing is known.
When the door opens to this strange realm
Be ready to listen;
Let it guide your head and your hand
For who knows what treasures will rise up to be recorded.
Do not question why it happens or how it happens;
Act as the scribe bringing news from hidden regions,
From deep recesses beyond our knowing.
Listen, listen to the faint breezes or the dark storms
Blowing in from the land beyond this world.

Ode to Friendship

I sing a song in praise of friendship,
Of long conversations with people of like mind,
Of laughter and tears,
Of history going back years.
I sing of the community of companions,
Of slow meals and cups of tea,
Of the tossing round of ideas,
The exchange of experiences.
I sing of the sharing of good times
And the sharing of bad times —
Of a shoulder to cry on —
Of hands to be held, supported and supporting.
Love has been praised endlessly
But friendship has been forgotten.
Today I celebrate my friends
And all the ties that hold us together.

Happiness

I am having a time of great happiness.
I do not understand how it has come upon me.
It crept silently up on little soft feet
So that I hardly noticed its approach.
Where has it come from
After my long years of mourning and loneliness?
I have a bubbling inside of more than contentment.
All is right with me and my world.

My Rock

Here I am, visiting my poetry rock after more than a year.
The tide is rising
And the surf is washing up around its base.
My rock is like a tiny island on which I sit
Surrounded by swirling water.
The ocean is rough and grey
And a cold southerly wind hits against my face.
I am here alone at my beach house
And revelling in my aloneness.
I can do what I like when I like,
And it pleases me to sit on my rock
And watch the wild Pacific throwing itself at the shore.
Ah, rock, you have comforted me often in times of anguish —
Now you are here for me
In the time of my pleasure and my strength.

Exultation

Do not walk around with a dull face looking at the ground;
Do not invite death to be your constant companion;
Do not live in fear at stepping out and being seen
But exult at existing.
Exult at the miracle of frogs and kangaroos;
Exult at the sun rising every morning
And at the waxing and waning of the moon;
Exult at loving in the face of violence and destruction –
Remember always, the exultation!

Wedding Poem

for Anne and my son, Kim

May these two, in linking their lives,
Stand by one another at all times —
In times of joy and times of sorrow —
In times of happiness and times of strife —
In times of contentment and times of danger.
May the many years to come
Deepen their understanding and their love.
Hand in hand, may they and theirs
Walk in growing strength and wisdom,
In enjoyment and prosperity
All the days of their lives.

Likenesses

When I look at my son's daughter
I see my own face in hers
Though she is as fair as I was dark.
When I look at my daughter's daughter,
I see my husband's face in hers.
By some miracle of genes
Our features have each been preserved in two of our grandchildren.
From how many forgotten ancestors did they come to us
And in how many descendants,
As yet unthought of and unborn,
Will they appear again and again,
Passing on down the generations
As long as humankind exists?

My Descendants

How will they lead their lives,
These descendants of mine, when I am dead?
Where will their destinies take them
In a time that I will never know?
Will they love and have children?
Will they find their life's work?
Will they be strong in body and soul?
Will they face suffering with strength?
O how I wish them goodness and blessings
For all the years of their lives.

Memories and Poems

Some day my daughter will be an old woman
And my son will be an old man
And I will be gone out of their lives.
All that will be left of me then will be their memories
And my poems to remind them of who I was.

Only Yesterday

After his father suddenly died,
My small son drew a picture with his crayons
And said to my friend:
"I can never, never show him my drawings any more."
When she told me this,
Tears sprang to my eyes as if it were only yesterday
Instead of thirty long years ago.

357

For Brian Syron*

He is not long for this world, my dear friend.
He is building his ship of death
For the journey that is coming
And warning those who love him of his departure.
He is leaving before his work is done
But those he taught will carry on his torch.
He has stood firm for his own dark people,
Giving his hand to those who needed help.
Tears will be shed
But all will praise the artist
Who poured his energy into his life
And enriched the lives of many
With his warmth and his laughter.
His ship of death lies waiting at the wharf.
Goodnight, sweet prince,
And flights of angels sing thee to thy rest.

Aboriginal actor, director and teacher. Man of the Biripi Tribe.

Ghosts of Sydney

Walking in this park on the edge of the harbour,
I came upon two rock carvings made by the Kooris *
Long before this great city was thought of.
The dark hands that cut into the rock are gone and forgotten
And all the descendants of this harbour tribe are gone and forgotten,
Destroyed by the makers of this city.
Surely their ghosts must haunt these coves
Which were theirs for so many centuries
Before the white men came.

The Blue Mountains

What strange timeless spirit
Broods over these mountains and vast blue valleys?
What is the dreaming, unknown to me,
That is embedded in the great cliffs and rocks,
The peaks and the valleys?
The first people of this place
Have left these strange regions
Taking their myths and their ways with them,
But their dreaming still lies over the land.
How can I find a way to reach into the mystery of these mountains?

* *Australian Aborigines*

Ode for Women Readers

O woman, you who are reading these words,
Never forget the enslavement of women
Down the centuries and even still, today.
Do not forget the dying in childbirth,
The dying of the babies and the children;
The beatings endured, the incest, the shame,
The bound feet and the bound minds.
O woman, do not forget your heritage of horror and of fortitude
Of the women who bore our forebears.
Do not forget, also, the loving and the nurturing,
The strength and the bravery and the endurance.
O woman, remember those who were enslaved
And never become an enslaver;
Remember the anguish of the mothers
And treasure your compassion —
Never let your heart harden and become cold.
O woman of today,
Pass on your freedom to your daughters
And your daughters' daughters.

David and Goliath

She is living with an internal dragon
That has been ruling her for fifty years.
Now the real contest has begun
And the challenge has been accepted.
She has to rally all her strength
To defeat this creature that comes from who knows where —
Her past, her family, her own expectations.
To discover that she is David,
And that no one but she can defeat her own Goliath,
Takes a courage that few possess.

Homage to Mothers

What is the heart-link that ties mothers to their children
For all of their lives?
The mother grows these tiny beings out of her own body,
Bears them,
Feeds them,
Watches over them, their walking and their talking,
Washes them,
Protects and loves them
And nurtures them with her soul.
Then, suddenly, in such a short time,
It is all over and they are gone,
Grown up and away
And off on the adventure of their own lives.

All hail to mothers
Who are blamed and criticised,
Resented and rebelled against
But without whom not one of us would exist.

Mother and Child

A child is knitted into the very fabric of a mother's being
Until she dies.
The child, as it grows older,
Is busy undoing the ties to its mother
So that it can cast free
Like a ship leaving its wharf for the open seas.
It does not look back
For fear of seeing the pain and the tears left behind
Just when it is stretching its wings to fly.

My Kitchen

I have neglected my kitchen for years,
Keeping the benches clean,
The washing up and the cooking done
But ignoring the paint peeling off the walls
And the cupboards choked with old jars of dead beans
And decayed substances that I could not identify.
Living alone
I had other things to do
Than worry about the state of my kitchen.
Then, suddenly, I could stand it no more;
I had to have it painted and tidied
And a pleasure to be in.
After the painting, came the clearing out —
The emptying of jars —
The washing of the cupboards —
The throwing out of the accumulation of useless things
I had saved in case I needed them.
Now my kitchen shines white in its new paint
And is decorated with beautiful objects.
My cupboards are tidy —
Some are even empty
And I know where everything is.
Now, when I prepare a meal,
I stand and admire the order and splendour
Of my newly-shining kitchen.

Night Walking

I often go walking around the streets at night
Whilst my timid neighbours lock themselves in their houses
Afraid to venture out.
I rarely meet anyone on my way but as I go
I wonder who lives in these little old houses.
Sometimes I have a glimpse of lighted rooms
Cosy with books and lamps and chairs;
I catch the scent of flowers in the gardens,
Then I walk home to my books and my bed and my dreams.

Old Places

I sit in the car driving around the foothills of the Jura
And I cannot believe that I am here in Europe and not in Sydney.
I look at the vineyards,
At the chateaux,
At the cobbled streets,
At the villages and the grey stone houses
And feel the timelessness of the old places.
We, in our newness, have put utility and fashion before beauty
And throw up buildings without thought or plan.
I can see why my heart leans to these old places
Because they satisfy my soul.

Romainmôtier, Switzerland

I am sitting in a field of buttercups and large yellow dandelions,
Tiny white daisies and little mauve flowers.
There is the sound of waters from a small stream near me
And cows anxiously mooing to be milked.
I cannot see the village behind me,
The old stone church, the priory and the houses.
The tree-covered hills rise from the valley
Where I sit and draw under a blossoming apple tree.
I am having a day of sun and drawings and fun
With my artist friends.

Drunk with Drawing

On this strange painting trip
I am becoming drunk with drawing.
I have, in my life, been drunk with beauty,
Drunk with love,
Drunk with poetry
But never before have I been drunk with drawing.

Drawing

I sit in a street drawing an old house;
Cars go by and occasionally a person walks past.
I draw the verandah, the roof and the windows
And the houses behind going up the hill.
I take my time as there is no hurry,
My mind on the shapes and the shadows and the tones.
This is one of my lovely times
When I leave the world of doings to draw.

Flying Home

Peeping out of the window of the plane at 3 a.m.
Whilst all the other passengers lay sleeping,
I saw the moon like a golden boat sailing along
As it rose over the edge of the world.

A Thought

"God can only set in motion; He cannot control the things he has made."

T'ao Ch'ien, 372-427A.D.

A novelist invents her characters
And then they take on a life of their own,
Not caring about their creator
Or what she wants them to do.
I wonder if this happened to God —
That after creating people
They took their lives into their own hands,
Doing what they wanted to do
Whilst God sat somewhere up there
Wringing His metaphorical hands
At what they have done and are still doing.

Evolution

I have been to the Natural History Museum
To see what the human race has evolved from,
But the real question I am faced with is –
Who can tell what we are evolving into?

I Met a Man

Last night
I met a man who would devour the whole world like an apple
If he could get his mouth around it.
He is right;
He is cold and without charm
And full of ambition.
I fear for our world with such people in high places.

Secrets

How many secrets have been kept over the years
And never spoken of?
Festering within, they enlarge like ulcers.
How many shames have been hidden?
How many humiliations endured?
How many actions or thoughts denied?
How many confessions have never been made?
How many others have been blamed to deflect the guilt of the guilty?
And how much of our inner selves have we secreted away through
    fear?
Rejoice! For the world is full of secrets.
Rejoice! For it is also full of truth
And the truth will prevail
For in our secrets is also the truth
Of who we are and what we are.

Stopping Places

For years, when I have driven alone to my beach house,
I have stopped by the roadside to write poems.
Now all my little stopping places are being eliminated
To improve the flow of traffic.
Someone in the traffic department does not understand
The need for poets to drive slowly,
To catch poems as they float by
And to have stopping places to write them down
Before they disappear into the air like dreams.

Thoughts for Felix Mendelssohn

I am driving through the mountains as the summer sun is setting.
There is a stillness in the air
And the frenzy of Christmas has passed.
I listen to a symphony by Mendelssohn as I drive
And I think how surprised he would be by cars and tape decks
And a woman driving herself across the country in her own vehicle
And listening to his music
At the late end of the twentieth century.

New Year

All this holiday week at my beach house
We have been surrounded by birds and bird song –
Rainbow lorikeets, magpies, currawongs and honey eaters;
And then flocks of pink and grey galahs
Like bunches of pink flowers in the trees.
What messages from the gods up there
Are these birds bringing for this year so newly with us?

Beach House II

The thin walls of this house hold out the Weather
And the roof holds off the rain and the storm
But the windows let in the sun and the light
And the dark of the night.
Into this house are built the seeds of creation –
Novels, poems, paintings, friendship and love.
It is a house of the soul –
A house of healing –
A house of truth –
A house of calmness.
This little grey house hidden amongst the dark casuarinas
On the edge of its cliff
Has a secret and amazing life that only its dwellers know.

These Last Years

What does the spirit say in these last years of my life
When the world is in such turmoil?
Be strong and be calm in the midst of frenzy;
Listen and look and say what has to be said;
Do not be overcome with fear
For you are held in the hands of the living God;
Do not feel alone
For you walk the path all the poets have walked
And have their words for your comfort;
Keep your heart open despite the pain
And love those you love;
Hold out your hands to those who are lost
For they need to be found;
Stand always for justice and mercy;
Pour your heart into your poems
For the whole of living is a continuous poem;
See the eternal through the transitory;
See the large in the small
And the small in the large
And never forget laughter and enjoyment.
That is what the spirit says in these,
The last years of my life.

Await the Spring, 1998

Poet

Who can tell why I was given the gift of poetry?
I received it early from the muse
But I was too young and too ignorant to nurture it.
I turned away, entranced instead
By trying to remake the world.
It was finally grief and love
That shattered me into becoming a poet —
That started me listening to the voice within
Which I had, for so long, refused to hear.
At last I was fulfilled and full of grace,
Fruitful with words forming into poems.
The muse had knocked at my door
But it took twenty years
Before I opened it and let her in.

First Born

Seventy five years ago, in a suburb of Melbourne,
A child was born.
There were no special stars in the sky at the time
And there were no wise men about
To be interested in the birth —
There were too many ordinary children
Being born everywhere
For anyone except her own family to care.
Unbeknownst to the child,
She arrived on the Passover, Easter and the equinox.
I was that child, first born,
Fashioned by security,
Fashioned by death and tears,
Moulded by the times I grew up in,
Depression, war and prosperity
And by dreams and books and love.
I never thought I would become a poet
And, surprisingly enough, a mother as well.
I have lived now for three quarters of a century —
So long and yet, in the history of the universe,
Not more than a few seconds.
I look back and read my life like a fascinating novel
And wonder what will be the end of my story.

Auntie Tillie

I write today for my Auntie Tillie
Who inhabited my childhood and my growing up
And whom the family said I took after.
When I knew her she was tall and thin and stooped,
With a long narrow face and straight short hair.
She wore little round spectacles and strange hats
And had never been beautiful.
She had lived for many years
In a small room in a boarding house,
Existing on a tiny income left by her father.
She was mad about music.
Family tradition had it
That she could have become a concert pianist
But no respectable girl
Could do such a thing in those days
So her piano lessons were discontinued.
She was short sighted
So she secretly used a pair of glasses to see
Until her mother confiscated them —
No one would many a plain girl in spectacles
And no one did, even without them.
She wrote poems and stories and a novel
Which were never published;
She wrote letters to the newspapers which were.
She was intelligent and clever with crossword puzzles
And entertained the boarders where she lived
Playing Chopin and Beethoven.
She spent her days with her two sisters and my brothers and me
And, at ninety four, fell down the stairs, broke her hip,
And went to hospital for the first time in her life.
She lingered on for several years and then she died,
Glad to go from a life that had been too long and too unfulfilled.
I sing of my Auntie Tillie,

Pitied by the family because she was an old maid,
But loved by me.
She would have been the only one
Who would have rejoiced that I, her only niece, became a poet.

Old Friends — New Friends

Old friends, old friends
Take me back through the history of my life
To times that I remember
And to times I would as soon forget.
I hold my old friends to my heart —
They are more steady than lovers.
New friends, new friends
Come into my life
Opening my eyes to new ideas, new activities —
Overturning outworn routines and habits
With excitements and surprises.
I need both the old and the new
To carry me on to wherever I am going.

Rare Souls

Some people have sharp corners in their personalities
That you bump into as you pursue their friendship;
Others have palpable walls around themselves for protection
But here and there are a few who have no walls or corners.
They are rare, these open ones,
Hidden amongst the ordinary folk.
When you are lucky enough to discover some,
Treasure and cultivate them
For you have discovered rare souls
Who will enrich your life.

Migrants

Newcomers to this old land
Have to grow new roots,
Have to grow into their adopted country;
Perhaps they never will
If they have left their hearts behind.
Perhaps it is only their children
And their children's children
Who will truly belong
To this place where they were born;
Then, having no memories of the old places
From whence their people came,
They will be foreigners forever
In the lands of their forefathers.

Australia Day

On this day in 1788
The conquerors of this land arrived in little ships
With their cargo of convicts and Christianity.
Little did the Kooris* know
That their fate was sealed,
That they would be more despised than the convicts,
That guns and poison would decimate their tribes
As their land was taken from them.
Let us not forget today
That we began as a prison
And, as conquerors of a people,
Doing all the cruel things
That conquerors have always done
To those they have conquered.
Let us not be complacent
As our reparations to these first Australians
Have only just begun.
On this Australia Day
We still have far to go.

* *The name aborigines of South-Eastern Australia call themselves.*

383

Sea Mist over Sydney

I watched the white sea mist
Creep like a huge winged dragon
Over Manly and the cliffs of North Head,
Up over the slopes of Balmoral
And down across the harbour waters.
The hot air cooled and dampened.
Now the mist nearly filled the harbour.
I can only see the tops of the Opera House sails
And the bridge has all but disappeared.
The setting sun is trying to shine through the fog;
The south shore of the harbour
Has faded away into a grey shadow
And ships are sounding their foghorns.
I sit on a headland watching and listening,
Pierced by a fierce love
For this city of mine.

The Old Tribes

Tonight, after my solitary meal,
I had to leave the house and go down to the water,
To the park at the edge of the harbour,
To walk in the light of the setting sun,
And listen to the water lapping on the rocks.
The tall city buildings are softened in the summer mist.
The busy harbour is empty of boats and ships
And calm in the cool of the evening.
I sit alone on the large rocks watching the water
Just as the old tribes must have done for thousands of years,
Fishing and swimming and gathering shellfish.

Sydney

Today my city is covered in smog,
The city buildings, the harbour, the houses, the trees
Are wrapped in a white film like muslin,
Beautiful but dreadful.
If we are not more caring
We will choke ourselves in our own terrible emissions.

Mystery

I feel a poem on the tip of my tongue
As I turn my bed lamp off to sleep.
I close my eyes and snuggle down in the warmth.
The poem niggles in my mind
And I open my eyes and write.
The mother of my friend
Is preparing to leave this world;
Only her poor wasted body is left.
Her spirit has already gone.
Living so long has become a misery
But she is too afraid to die.
Give her good courage for the journey.
Here is my poem of sleeping and dying
And of the mystery of it all.

Braidwood

I am sitting by the open fire
As it burns down to a heap of glowing coals.
All the evening we have been warm and cosy,
Adding logs and poking the fire into flame
When it burnt low,
Enjoying the country luxury of a real fire.
Outside the house lie the bush and the hills,
Cold and dark in the approaching winter,
But we are inside with plenty of firewood,
Golden flames, talk and the enjoyment of friends.

Goanna

I met a long grey goanna in the bush today
As I sat drawing a scribbly gum.
She waddled across the clearing on her splayed legs,
Flicking her tongue and exploring for food.
She walked carefully around me,
Throwing me glances now and again,
Then came up close to inspect this strange being
Sitting quite still with a bit of stick in her hand.
Then she circled me again, quite unafraid,
And wandered off into the bush.
I do not know what she thought of me
But I thought how beautiful her spots and stripes,
Her shape and walk
And how ancient she looked
Just like this land on which we both live.

Country Road

As we drove along the country road
I saw two trees covered in white shining blossoms.
As we drew nearer
I saw they were a-flower
With a whole clan of white cockatoos
Quietly sitting in the branches
In the early morning sun.

My Travelling Companion

There is a tiny spider that lives on my car.
It makes a little web across the outside mirror;
Each time I wipe it off
It weaves a new one to replace it.
It is a most persistent and travelled spider;
It drives with me all over Sydney,
To Canberra and back
And up the coast to my beach house.
I usually dislike spiders, especially large ones,
But I am becoming quite fond
Of this little travelling companion of mine.

Shoalhaven River

Sitting by the river bank in the bush
All I can hear is the low music of the water
Flowing in little waterfalls over the rocks of the footway.
The water is icy and the rocks slippery
And I dare not cross for fear of falling
And hurting my injured back.
The river is low in the drought;
The trunks of the scribbly gums
Are white in the sunlight
And reflected in the shallow river pool;
Big bunchy clouds are floating by in the sky;
There is snow on the distant Brindabellas
And I await the spring to heal my ailing body
And give me back my freedom.

The Old Road

I drive home slowly along the old road
And I remember the years we drove this road together,
Talking companionably or being silent,
Practising our Chinese conversation together,
Laughing and enjoying each other's company.
I think back further to our children's childhoods
When this was the only way north
And we drove it with my children and yours
Through traffic jams and car sickness,
Arguments and games.
I love this slow old road
Through the bush and the mountains,
Over the river and its valley
And the many memories it brings back to me.

Christmas Eve, 1994

Tonight I sit alone in my house
Listening to the rain outside
And remember other Christmas eves
With those I loved who are now dead
And with my children who are now parents
With their own children and far from here.
The past has crept over me
Like a cold fog rolling in from the sea
And I am full of memories and tears
For the years that have gone.

Fiery Summer

It was a wild old night on top of our cliff.
The wind was roaring around the house
And at the foot of the cliff
The sea was raging against the rocks.
The noise woke me and I lay awake
Listening to the uproar.
It was cold after the heat of the day
With the wind dashing in the window
And I pulled the blanket up around my shoulders.
Winter is coming at last
After the hottest and fieriest summer
That I remember.

Approaching Storm

The lake is still;
Dark storm clouds are approaching;
The white paperbarks beside the lake
Are reflected in the water;
Small brown ducks are floating about
And I hear pale thunder behind the hills.
The clouds move closer
And I await the breaking of the storm.

Anguish

I have a blank page in front of me.
What shall I write on it?
Write that I am growing old;
Write that I am overcome with grief
At the thought of dying —
At that moment I will lose all I love,
All that is familiar —
My children and their families;
The friends I will leave behind;
My old house full of my treasures and my books;
I will lose my poetry, the sea and beauty
And I will lose my body,
That old friend who has carried me all these years.
I will lose my eyes that have seen so much,
My mind that has thought so much —
All, all will be gone.
I know only too well
The anguish of losing those I have loved
But I have yet to discover
The anguish of leaving all that I love.

Poetry Rock

Today my poetry rock is surrounded by sand;
Sometimes when I come and the tide is high,
It is surrounded by turbulent water.
Sometimes it is one large rock
In the midst of many rocks
When the ocean has swept the deep sand
To the other end of the beach.
Whatever the weather or the season or the tides,
My rock is there
Waiting for me to visit it
And always giving me a new poem to take home.

The Whale

Today my beach was visited by a whale.
Everyone stood and stared
At this great mammal gambolling in the sea.
It rolled on its side flicking its huge tail,
Spouted water in the air,
Then raised its dark head out of the sea
As if it were standing on its tail
And surveyed the admiring crowd on the shore.
Spellbound I stood and watched it at its water play,
This enormous creature of the seas,
Come to visit us,
The small creatures of the land.

Flight

There are four large sea birds
Flying and swooping far out over the sea.
Are they playing or courting or hunting —
Or flying and looping just for the sheer joy of their flight?

Paris III

Paris in the autumn in the sun.
The Luxembourg Gardens are crowded with people
Strolling and running,
Doing Tai Chi and martial arts under the trees;
Children having pony rides;
Sunbakers and readers on the old iron chairs
And my friend and I walking amongst them.
Why did I come to Paris again?
What is the fascination of this city?
Why does it draw me like a magnet?
Now that I am here it is like coming home;
I am no longer a stranger from a far country
But I have begun to belong —
To love the narrow cobbled streets, the boulevards;
The rows of mad chimney pots on top of the old buildings;
The wrought-iron balconies;
The bistros and little restaurants;
The people of Paris
And the special throbbing excitement of the city.
I love my own sun-drenched city of the south —
Queen of the cities of the sea —
And I love Paris —
Queen of the cities of the north.

Traveller into Homebody

The traveller has returned from her travels over the world.
She has flown back to her house in the south
And there has turned into a homebody
Instead of a traveller.
She picks flowers from her garden for vases on her
        table —
Nasturtiums, jonquils, camellias;
She gathers mandarins and grapefruit from her trees
To eat and make into marmalade;
She shops at the local shops,
Swims in the harbour every day,
Works with her clients,
Lies on her couch now and again
To rest and to read
And visits with friends for talk and for tea.
Her life has shrunk into a small compass.
She is delighted, now, to potter about at home
Instead of travelling the world.

Books

Ever since I learned to read
I have been greedily gobbling up books
As if they might all disappear
Before I got my hands on them.
Growing up, I did not want toys or dolls
But only books.
The first money I ever earned
Sent me into a bookshop
To buy more of my paper treasures.
Now I have a house full of books,
Bulging bookcases in every room,
And I add to the numbers
By writing more myself.
What a delightful passion to have
That has lasted all my life
And given me such pleasure and satisfaction.

The Skull

I have been living with a skull for four months.
I have drawn it at different angles;
I painted it in blues and creams
Standing on a royal blue cloth,
The light falling on the bones of the face,
The rest in shadow.
I wonder who he was,
Where did he come from
And how did he die?
What sights did he see through the eyes
That filled those eye-sockets?
What did he eat with those teeth
Still set so firmly in the jawbones?
What did he smell with that nose that has gone?
What words did he speak
With lips and tongue that are dust?
Alas, poor Yorick, I, too, will end like you
But now, while I live,
I draw skulls and write poems.

I Sleep Alone

I sleep alone in this large house
In the dark, in the silence,
Under the night sky
Or in the light of the moon.
I sleep alone
Wishing sometimes for someone to share my bed,
To hold me in their arms,
To stroke my head,
To whisper to me in the night.
Through the winter and the spring,
The summer and the autumn
I sleep alone in this old house.

Imprisoned

I sit on the ground
In the dim cave of my aloneness,
My memories crowding around me like milling shadows,
Dark and full of grief,
And I cannot move.
I am like a person in prison;
I cry out for help and nobody answers
For aloneness muffles my cries.
Who can I talk to in this desolate place
Where there are no companions,
No locked cell, no barred doors
But in which I am imprisoned?

The Unconscious

Do not venture, even inadvertently,
Into the hidden depths of the unconscious
Without a guide who is familiar
With the dangers of such a journey.
The waters of the unconscious may seem calm and inviting
For the solitary explorer
But the dangers are hidden —
Wild currents that can sweep the unwary swimmer
Into deep and drowning waters —
Tangling weeds that are like arms
Waiting to clasp the unwatchful.
Do not venture into such unsafe waters
Without a guide who can take you by the hand
And lead you safely through this fateful place.

The Old Language

Will poetry lose its power
If people forget the old language
And the old words?
This is the time of computers and internet
And television
And the new language of machines.
I hope that poems of the heart and passion
Will not be drowned
In the cold waves of technology.

Worshipping Words

I, who have always worshipped words,
Am losing them in my old age.
They fly out of my head like darting birds
While I search for them,
Then fly back when they are ready.
What a horror for a writer
If they never ever returned.

Monstrous Creature*

When I came home at dusk
There was a large grey tarantula
Sitting on the door jamb beside the keyhole.
How was I to get into the house
Past this monstrous creature?
We looked at each other, both afraid,
I, of this large long-legged spider by my door
And she, of the huge giant
Who had so suddenly appeared.
She summed up my murderous intent,
Slipped sideways, folding up her hairy legs
And quickly squeezed herself
Into a small crack behind the door jamb
And disappeared —
Then I was free to enter my house
And lock the spider safely out.

* *Erroneously called tarantulas by most Australians, they are actually*
  Huntsman spiders and are harmless.

Gymea Lily

I have filled a flower-pot with earth
And planted in it seeds of the Gymea lily
Hoping that they will grow.
I love the flaring red
Of these wild lilies of the bush,
Eight or ten feet high
On their long green stems,
Like a huge bouquet of scarlet flowers.
I have watered them carefully
And put them in the sun
But all that has grown so far
Is a tiny tomato plant.

Watch Over Me

Cover me with darkness, night,
And let me slide into dreams.
The sea is calm and the breeze is light.
Angels, beings of the air,
Watch over me
And keep me safe as I sleep.

Ancestors: Old Melbourne Cemetery

When I was a little girl
My grey-haired grandmother
Brought me to this cemetery every month
To visit the graves of her parents.
That was before I knew what death was.
I was too young to understand her grief
Or to ask the questions I now want answered.
Now, over seventy years later,
I come to this cemetery with my own daughter
To find my grandparents.
We search until we stumble on the graves
And there they lie, side by side,
Sophia and Henry, dying within a year of one another,
And leaving me so bereft that, even today,
I have buried the memories of their going.
There, beside them, are the graves of my great grandparents
Whom I never knew,
Who came to this country in their youth
And died in the fullness of their years.
I, who came to this cemetery as a child,
Am now a grey-haired grandmother myself,
Stirring with memories,
And telling my daughter stories of her ancestors.
Will she, in her turn,
Bring her children to visit my grave
When I, too, in the fullness of my years,
Have left this fortunate life?

Golden Years

These are the golden years of my life —
These years that I never thought to reach.
I feared that seventy was over the hill,
That I was on the downward run
To deterioration and senility;
But how much better this is than my youth —
That young girl I remember
Who was so full of loneliness and shyness,
Who felt so different and never fitted in,
Even into her own family.
I have travelled far from that distant time
And here I am at seventy three
Strong and vigorous,
Full of interests and confidence,
Pleased that I do not fit in and never will,
Loving my family and friends
And writing poems that please my heart.

A Fortunate Star, 2001

Whisper of the Waves

We sat in the shade of the verandah drinking coffee
And discussing painting and writing poetry
While we listened to the sea
Washing up on the sand far below.
From this old house on the hill
We looked through the branches
Of the tall gum trees
And the steep path down to the beach.
It could have been 1920 or 1950
But it was 1997.
It was as if we were outside time;
It could have been Greece in Socrates' day;
It could have been Matthew Arnold on Dover Beach;
It could have been Whitman on Paumanok's grey shore,
But it was today and in Sydney
And my little white car waited for us in the street.
The rush and push of the city was invisible to us
In this time of talking of painting and poetry
Above the white beach
And the whisper of the waves.

Spring

This is the seventy-ninth spring of my life.
When I was a child
I did not notice the spring;
When I was a young woman
I had other things on my mind.
But now spring is a celebration —
Another year has been given to me
Full of blossoms and flowers.
How many more springs will I see
Before the seasons of this world
Will no longer matter to me?

Auntie Tillie and Me

When I was a little girl
My mother said to me:
"Stand up straight —
Put your shoulders back
Or you will end up
Just like your Auntie Tillie."
I, of course, took no notice.
My Auntie Tillie was thin and tall and old.
She walked everywhere
Hunching over her shoulders as she went.
Now, today, I walk hunched over
Just like her,
Just as my mother predicted that I would
All those years ago.

On Revisiting Melbourne

How comfortably I fit into this city of my childhood
And growing up.
I slide into it
As if the fifty years since my leaving
Do not exist.
I love the familiarity of the streets and the trees,
The green trams in which I rode
To university and to work each day.
The little old houses
And the large Victorian mansions
Still stand as I remember them.
There are new glass buildings, expressways, underpasses
But it is still my city.
Although I have a life elsewhere
And am only a visitor now
I feel that here I have come home.

Sydney

Today the tall glass buildings of my city
Are wreathed in cloud
And the rain is greying the colours of water and trees.
The harbour is dark and dull
And the cars on the roads drive slowly
With their lights on in the gloom.
I drive carefully through the traffic,
Glad that my destiny brought me to this place
Where sea and land, harbour and bush meet
And where I have the ocean at my feet.

Who Is It?

As I passed a shop mirror this morning
I caught a glimpse of this strange old woman,
With wild grey hair, walking past.
She had a strong look,
Rounded shoulders and wrinkled eyes.
I looked again and thought
I have changed into someone I do not recognise;
I have grown old, it seems,
And not noticed it was happening.

My Brothers and I

How is it that my brother and I
Were born under a fortunate star
With the gift of enjoyment and optimism
And yet our youngest brother,
Born under a more fateful star,
Chose failure and death before his time?
Who can give an answer to such a question?
Who can question the fate of any individual,
Even one's own brother?

Friends

I was an alone child
In the midst of mother and father,
Brothers, grand parents,
Aunts and many cousins.
I was an alone girl at school
Until I found a friend
And discovered the joys of friendship.
Ever since I have found more friends
And never tire of the joys of togetherness.

Ink

Today coming down the expressway
On my way home
I passed what I thought was a petrol tanker
But to my surprise
It was full of printers' ink.
How many millions of words as yet unwritten
Are in that huge tank.
It make thousands of books and magazines and newspapers —
All will be conjured out of that black ink
Swishing away inside that tanker that I passed today.

Storm

I am caught in the fury of a storm,
Lightning and thunder right overhead
And rain so heavy that I cannot continue driving.
In the middle of the afternoon
It is dark as if night had fallen.
I have stopped my car because I cannot see.
Will I turn and go back home
Or will I continue when the storm eases?
The lightning flashes all around,
The thunder shakes the ear.
I cannot go back and I cannot go forward.
I sit marooned in the wild flood of water and sound
And wonder if the gods are showing their anger
At the desecration of our land.

Driving

What is more exciting
Than driving alone
Out of the crowded city
Into the country and the bush?
The only better thing
Is to drive with a friend
To chat with and laugh with
And talk of deep things
And light things
And stop for cups of tea
In delightful companionship.

Stranger

I am a stranger living in a strange world;
I am a poet living in an unpoetic time;
I am like a fish out of water
Gasping in unfriendly air.
How can I find nourishment in such circumstances?
I am choking in the shallowness
And narrowness surrounding me;
I am being decimated by those who are destroying poetry;
I am drowning in false values, sentimentality and fashion
How can I nurture myself and save my soul?

The Art Gallery of New South Wales, Sydney

I have been to the Art Gallery
To see some art
But what l saw was a large wall
Filled with flashing red numbers,
Signifying what?
I saw milk crates tumbled about
With turdish lumps of coloured plastic inside them.
I saw a dead tree on the floor
Wrapped up in old canvas.
There are no rules anymore —
Anything goes
As long as it is new and gimmicky.
I do not want to look at such meaningless nonsense
So I go into the Oriental Room
And feast my eyes on the calmness and beauty
Of ancient Chinese art.

The Julian Ashton Art School, Sydney

I love this art school
Over one hundred years old
And being run by the great grandson of its founder.
The studios are untidy —
With plaster casts of skulls and skeletons,
Heads of the famous and the unknown,
All to be drawn by the aspiring artists.
There are dozens of easels and drawing boards,
Drapes for the models, still lifes
And all the other paraphernalia
That art students need.
Young men and women mingle with the retired,
All earnest in their pursuit of art.
There are classes and teachers filling the studios
All day and half the night.
I stand at my easel
Struggling to draw a model.
Sounds of the city drift in the windows
Into the ordered chaos of the school.

Major's Creek

I am sitting at the side of a road
In this abandoned gold mining town,
Drawing an old tumbledown house.
This town was once thriving
With hotels and shops and excited gold diggers;
Now it has one small pub,
A landscape pitted with old diggings,
Not one shop, not even a school
And all day not one car has passed me.
What a contrast to life in Sydney,
Full of cars and trucks,
Millions of people frenziedly living in it,
While I sit here in this little village
Contentedly drawing in the sun.

Double Numbers

This year my daughter turns forty-four,
My friend turns fifty-five,
My cousin has turned sixty-six
And I have just turned seventy-seven.
What a lovely bunch of doubles.
I think I like being seventy-seven—
It feels a good number and a good year.
I cannot believe I am that old
When I only feel thirty-three.
My next double is eighty-eight.
Will I reach it and if I do,
How will it feel?

Travelling

It is so easy each night to get into bed,
Read a little,
Close my eyes
And travel into the country of my dreams.
The real countries are harder to reach;
Confined uncomfortably in a plane
Unable to sleep
And the mind silly in the high altitude;
Waiting in airports with crowds of other travellers
All flying in different directions.
Why do I travel the world in discomfort and danger
When I can reach my country of dreams each night
At no cost and in such comfort?

Drawing in France

I am making pictures every day
With pencil and with pen,
Drawing little villages, churches,
Fields on the rolling hills.
I am drawing people in cafes
Eating and drinking.
I am drawing without thinking
Now my hand is more practised.
I have a pleasure in it
That I cannot even describe.
Me and a pen and a drawing book
And a subject that intrigues me
And every moment of the years of practice
Join together into fruition and joy.

Singing Sunflowers, Burgundy

Over the hills and below the autumn skies
Great fields of wilted sunflowers
Stand in rows
Like thousands of withered soldiers
With bowed brown heads.
As the wind sweeps through them,
They sway and sing a low rattling song
To the listening sky and to me.

Graveyard in France, Bussière-sur-Ouche

I climb past the graves of the mothers and the fathers,
The children and the grandparents,
To the graves of the seven men
Lying high on the hill.
They lie in a row,
Dead at nineteen and twenty, twenty-two and twenty-five.
Fifty-two years they have lain on this alien hill —
Airmen, crashed with their bomber in 1943,
Buried by the villagers
And one of them my countryman.
Tears fill my eyes for these young men
Who gave their lives so generously
Far from their families and homes
And never returned.
The villagers honour them each year
And I, having no flowers to bring,
Honour them with fresh leaves;
I place a stone for remembrance
On the headstone of my compatriot
And take his memory back with me
To his distant homeland.

Lake Geneva
(For Eveline and Judy)

I am so full of the beauty of today
That I Cannot sleep.
The vineyards stretch down to the edge of the lake
And up the steep slopes to the sky;
The lake lies still like pale blue silk
Across to the mountains of France.
The little villages nestle in the sun
Amongst the ridges of the vines.
In the midst of grape growing and wine making
I was not drunk with wine
But with the beauty that surrounded me.
My mind goes over and over it in pleasure
And I cannot sleep.

Cosmic Rays, Museum at CERN,* Geneva

Every moment of every day
The universe out there
Is bombarding us with cosmic rays.
Unbeknownst to me until now
They are shooting through me day and night
And have been all my life.
These rays of nothingness or somethingness,
Zipping haphazardly through everything
Link us to the unknown universe out there.
How can I come to terms
With the enormity of the cosmos
And the invisible rays
That make us part of it?

*CERN: Organisation Européenne pour la Recherche Nucléaire. European
Organisation for Nuclear Research.

Noyers-sur-Serein, Burgundy

Sitting in my car
I was drawing this medieval town,
My attention on the lines of the roofs,
The angles of the tower
When suddenly I was hurtled back
To my childhood home
And my teenage years.
Floating out of the radio had come a song
And there was my cousin Nancy
Training to be the opera singer
She never became,
Singing that song to me.
Now, sixty years later,
It was as if it were yesterday.
It is many years since her voice was silenced
But she brought the music into my life
That has never failed me to this day.

Where are they now?

Where are they now
All those people I knew as a child?
Deep in the silence of the grave they lie
Mouldering in earth or consumed by fire—
Dust to dust, but what comes after?
Have their bodies fallen away
To mingle with earthly atoms
And is that all?
Or have their spirits left and risen —
But where?
To Nirvana?
To the Kingdom of the Jade Emperor?
To Heaven or to Hell?
To God?
Or do their souls fly to the spirit world
Where all is revealed?
Do they, at long last,
Discover the ultimate answer
Or is the ultimate answer unknowable?
Where have they gone
Those people whom I knew so many years ago?

Bush and Forest

Here at last is my beloved bush,
Dark and hard and prickly,
With twisted trees and branches
Dreaming on the hills and valleys;
Old man banksias,
Wattles just beginning to flower;
Tall red ash and dwarf apple gums,
With giant angophoras towering over them all.
How different is my bush
From the pale green forests of Europe
That I have just been walking through.

Bush Choir

As I wandered along the forest path
The chorus of cicadas in the trees
Nearly deafened me.
The sound softened and faded into silence,
Then again they raised their voices
To their highest pitch.
What kind of a chorus were they singing,
On and off, loud and soft,
And who is conducting this choir of thousands
In this green and lonely forest?

The Bee

The other day at my beach house
I found a bee drowning in my rain gauge.
Swimming and struggling and soaking wet,
It could not climb the slippery sides of the gauge.
I rescued it with a twig,
Putting it in the sun on my verandah.
With its tiny legs it wiped and wiped its head;
It shot its sting in and out;
It shook the water out of its fat little body
And combed its fur with its feet;
It pulled off the sodden yellow pollen from its legs
And spread out its wings to dry.
Then it flew off to its hive
To tell the other bees about its miraculous escape.

Cool Haven

My house is surrounded by trees.
In my back garden
The tiny liquidambar we planted years ago
Now towers above the house,
Shading it and keeping it cool in summer.
The grey olive has grown so large
It screens out the neighbouring flats.
In my front garden
I have a tall stately melaleuca,
Its white bark luminous at night,
And a red bottlebrush —
Both covered in bees
Humming amongst the cream and scarlet flowers.
In the comer of the garden near the street
Is a crabapple tree
Covered in the spring with pink and white blossoms.
All these trees are a delight to the flocks of lorikeets
Who come and chatter in my garden;
The trees shelter me,
Shade my house in summer
And on winter nights rustle their branches
And guide me into sleep.

Books

My house is full of books.
I have overloaded bookcases in nearly every room;
I have piles of books on every flat surface
All over the house.
I no sooner tidy some of them up
Than they overflow elsewhere.
Now I have discovered
That they are invading my bed.
If I am not careful
This flood of books will overwhelm me
And I will end up having to sleep on the floor.

In the Night

Sometimes when I am in bed at night
I hear sounds in the house —
Creaks or knocks or squeaks.
I listen, startled!
Is it a possum on the roof?
Or rats in the ceiling?
Or is it a board creaking?
Is there a burglar in the house?
I lie still and listen;
I am not really frightened
As the doors and windows are all locked.
Then silence returns
And I am safe again inside my house.

Sleep

O sleep,
Gather me up in your arms
And transport me to strange realms
Out of the everyday doings of my life
Into a place where anything can happen —
Where I can fly —
Where I can meet gryphons or dragons —
Become lost or found —
Sit in cars that drive themselves —
Talk to people who are dead
Or whom I have never met.
O sleep,
Gather me up in your arms
For the adventures of the night.

For Muir Holburn, died 16.11.1960

I had forgotten that today was your death day.
Thirty-six years is a long time.
For many years this day was a devastation;
Sometimes I wonder how I survived
Such a sudden and unexpected blow.
I lived because I had to live;
I had to live for our children —
I had to feed them and put them to bed;
I had to protect them and watch them grow;
I had to read to them and love them;
I had to repair my shattered soul.
Now that our children are parents
And I am even a great grandmother,
I have, at last, forgotten your death day.
Rest in peace wherever you are —
I remember so well all our time together
In the days of our youth —
You as lover, as husband, as friend
And as father of our children.

Partners
(For J.H. and J.G.)

I was glad
Spending the day with my friends in their house,
Learning maths, eating lunch, talking.
I was happy that they were happy –
Loving one another,
Being companionable,
Creating a new home, working,
Walking their dogs,
Talking to their cats
And being my friends
And yet I was sad –
Sad that I was alone
Having no partner any more
To share my life each day.
I left as night was falling,
Rain was falling,
Wind was blowing the trees
And the cold of winter was in the air.
I left, pleased with my day and my friends,
To eat alone in my house
And remember my happy days of partnering.

After the Second World War

I had thought that after seven years of war
Peace would be welcomed
And harmony would reign over all the lands.
Now, fifty years later,
The killing fields are full of bones and skulls
The killers still rampage
And innocents are still being slaughtered.

Uncivilized

For 40,000 years
This land was preserved and nurtured
By its inhabitants.
Since we, its new owners, invaded it
Two hundred years ago
We have polluted its rivers,
Degraded its soil,
Chopped down its forests,
Enslaved its previous owners
And call them uncivilized.

The Stolen Children*

Who can describe the agony of the mother
When her children are snatched away
Never to be seen again?
Who can know the agony of the father?
Who can feel the terror of the children,
Kidnapped by strangers
From the hearts of their families,
Put into orphanages far away
To be civilized and despised?
The whole terrible story has been hidden from us —
Now the children are grown
And telling their stories.
Listen to them!
Listen to the lost children and their mothers and fathers!
Weep with them
And ask forgiveness for the cruelty and despair
Which we, their conquerors, inflicted upon them.

* *"Indigenous children have been forcibly separated from their families and communities since the very first days of the European occupation of Australia."*

Bringing Them Home, 1997. p 27.

Evening

The lagoon is still at the end of the day;
The water is high
And lapping amongst the twisted roots
Of the pale paperbarks.
There are two children paddling along
In a blue canoe;
The sun is sinking
Behind the further shore.
White cockatoos are screeching and swooping
Over the surface of the water
In high excitement
Before they settle for the night.
I have eaten my evening meal
And come for a last walk
Before I, too, go home
And settle down for my night.

Lake George

Sheep are grazing on Lake George
Which has all but disappeared.
Its wide tranquil waters have become
A huge sheet of pale green grass.
Where has all that water gone
And when will it return
To flood the grassy plain
And become a lake again?

Scribbly Gums

This bush is full of old scribbly gums —
Some almost burnt through
In some past bushfire, but living still.
Some have shiny silver trunks,
Others are fawn or cream
And all are covered in scribbly messages.
What are they writing about?
What are these gums telling us?
Are they poems or short stories
Or bush ballads?
Or are they the autobiographies of the trees
That we, in our ignorance, are unable to read?

Sea Call

Sea memories in the bones and the cells;
Sea smells and seaweed;
Sound of the sea in ancient ears;
Salt water on the skin.
Like a magnet
The sea pulls me into its waiting waters.
I must be a sea thing become a land thing;
The sea is in my very core;
It still calls to me today
Through all the generations that have gone before.

Order and Chaos

I sit in my car
Watching the waves beating up the beach.
For how many aeons have they been washing up this shore?
I look at the sky,
Blue over the blue ocean,
And out to all the hidden galaxies
Of the unknown universe.
I look for the maker and shaker
Of the chaos and the order and the infinity.
I, in my car, am a little speck
In the face of this immensity and mystery,
Making tiny marks in ephemeral notebooks
And calling them poems.
I, who am here today and gone tomorrow,
Bow my head before the enormity and inevitability
Of all I see.

Eternity

When I was young
I took no heed of the end of my life —
I had eternity stretching in front of me.
Now that I am seventy-seven
Eternity has gone
And my end draws near.
I could live to ninety-three
Or I could die tomorrow;
I could live to eighty-four
Or just another year.
Uncertainty is my constant companion
But for some of the time I can still live
As if I have eternity
Stretching out in front of me.

Index

446

Index of First Lines

List of Drawings

Printed in Great Britain
by Amazon

60981245R00276